# NAPOLÉON
## An Intimate Portrait

Catalogue of the exhibition "NAPOLEON: An Intimate Portrait"

© 2005 Russell Etling Company
All photos © photo12.com-Pierre-Jean Chalençon
Additional photography by Virginia Wood Davis

ISBN: 0-615-13012-7

Published by Russell Etling Company
3621 Viscaya Court
Coral Gables, Florida 33134
www.napoleonexhibit.com

Printed in United States

Previous page
Portrait bust of Napoléon I
After Antoine-Denis Chaudet, with laurel crown by Pierre-Philippe Thomire. Porcelain
from Manufacture Imperiale de Sèvres — c 1810
Sèvres made about ten busts of Napoléon I, this being one of the largest.
Few survived, as Louis XVIII ordered their destruction.
Historical Provenance — Marshal Louis Alexandre Berthier collection
Bisque with gilded bronze

# NAPOLÉON
## An Intimate Portrait

A Traveling Exhibition from the Russell Etling Company
Featuring the Collection of Pierre-Jean Chalençon

—— Exhibition Catalogue Authors ——
Pierre-Jean Chalençon, Brett Topping and Russell Hull Etling
—— Catalogue Design ——
Natalie Brown

# Special Acknowledgements

For their additional support, we would like to thank:

House of Prelle

McGrane, Nosich & Ganz, P.A

Napoleonic Society of America

National Geographic Society

# Dedication

This exhibition is dedicated to the memory of the late Robert M. Snibbe, founder of the Napoleonic Society of America.

# Table of Contents

# A Message from the Exhibition Organizer

Since his appearance on the world stage, Napoléon Bonaparte (1769-1821) has been the object of intense public fascination. A brilliant military commander and visionary leader, he rose swiftly from obscurity to reign over a vast Empire…only to ultimately suffer crushing defeat, lonely exile and death on a remote and desolate island

With the 200th anniversary of Napoléon and Joséphine's coronation as Emperor and Empress of the French on December 2nd, 2004, we entered a period of renewed interest in this fascinating period and its central figure.

In recognition of this bicentennial and that of the decade-long imperial reign, Pierre-Jean Chalençon granted permission for our firm to mount an exhibition of his extraordinary collection of art and objects from the period and his vast array of personal possessions of Napoléon and those closest to him. Though elements of the collection have been loaned for major exhibitions around the world, this is the first time these irreplaceable artifacts have been seen in our continent.

As the son of a long-time "Napoléon buff," I grew up learning the story of this remarkable man. Through my father and my involvement with the Napoleonic Society of America, its publications, wonderful conferences and historic tours, I became an ardent enthusiast myself. The Society's late founder Robert M. Snibbe, to whom we dedicate this exhibition, always dreamed of the Chalençon Collection touring North America, for he believed that once people were exposed to these rare and intimate objects from Napoléon's personal world, they would be thirsty to learn more about him.

It is in that spirit that this exhibition has been developed. They say Napoléon ranks second only to Jesus as the subject of published biographies and papers, so we knew we couldn't possibly cover all there is to know about the Emperor's life and career. What we could do, though, was provoke our audience members to question what kind of man believes he can change the world and inspire them to learn more for themselves. We hope we've succeeded.

Russell Etling
President
Russell Etling Company

# A Message from the Collector

Napoléon Bonaparte – I heard that name for the first time when I was 8 years old. Now, almost thirty years later, the Emperor of the French is a daily part of my life.

It is an honor to share with you one of the largest private collections of Napoléon memorabilia in the world. Assembling it has been my privilege and my passion.

Why, though, has this figure from history held my complete interest all these years? In fact, it is the very contemporary nature of who he was that I find so enthralling. I see him as the first "modern" European leader - a truly "self-made" man, who rose to the seat of power without the aid of the royal lineage that had been required in France and across the continent for hundreds of years.

It is all the more fitting that we have premiered this exhibition in Washington, DC, the capital city of a nation that celebrates a person's ability to rise to leadership on the basis of his or her own ability and drive. Napoléon admired America and gave thought to making it his home after his fall.

The pieces in the exhibition have been selected not only for their great beauty and rarity, but also because they allow us to see into the heart of this extraordinary man. While a giant of history in the model of Alexander the Great, Julius Caesar and Charlemagne, he was also very human. He had great loves and was driven by his dreams for a better world, but was, at times, blind to the betrayal of others and the victim of his own flawed vision.

With over 250 items, many his own personal effects and treasures he gave to others, you will chart the course of his life – 52 years that changed the world. I believe no collection has ever been so close to the man.

May Napoléon Bonaparte fascinate you as much as he has fascinated me all these years.

Pierre-Jean Chalençon
President
Cercle France-Napoléon

# Exhibition Team

| | |
|---|---|
| EXHIBITION ORGANIZER | Russell Etling Company, Russell Etling, President |
| HEAD CURATOR | Pierre-Jean Chalençon |
| DESIGNER | Falconer Exhibits, Tonia Falconer Barringer |
| ASSOCIATE DESIGNER & EXHIBIT MANAGER | Mary Anna Murphy |
| MARKETING DIRECTOR | Natalie Brown |
| SCRIPT EDITOR | Brett Topping |

---

| | |
|---|---|
| ACCOUNTING SERVICES | Vega & Vega Associates |
| ARCHIVIST | Virginia Wood Davis |
| CASE DESIGN GRAPHICS | Viktor Deak |
| COLLECTION IMAGES | Photo12.com, Valérie-Anne Giscard d'Estaing, President and CEO |
| DOCUMENT REVIEW | Matthew J. Valcourt, Esq. |
| FINE ARTS HANDLING | David White |
| FLORAL DESIGN | Ann Hull Etling |
| INSURANCE SERVICES | Morton D. Weiner/AMPAC, Inc., Jeff B. Weiner |
| | Ross & Yerger, Dudley D. Wooley, CPCU, CIC |
| LEGAL SERVICES | McGrane, Nosich & Ganz, P.A., James J. Nosich, Esq. and George Daven Sirejian, Esq. |
| PERIOD FABRIC RECREATIONS | House of Prelle, Maryse Dusoulier, Director of Communication, and |
| | Philippe Conzade, Upholstery |
| PHOTO MURAL PRODUCTION | National Geographic Society |
| PRODUCTION SUPPORT | Charles H. Bessant; Charles Bob Bryen; Anthony Florido; Iris Fuentes; Carlos Plaza |
| PUBLIC RELATIONS | Alys Daly |
| TEXT REVIEW | Douglas Allen; Tina Banner; Eric Morgenthaler |
| TRANSLATIONS | Jade Translations, LLC, Janine De Ruyver |
| TRANSPORTATION LOGISTICS | Mallory Alexander, LeRoy Pettyjohn |
| | Vulcan Fret Services, Pierre Gosse |
| VIDEO PRODUCTION | Wilson & Associates, Michael A. Wilson |
| WEB DESIGN | Brooks Weisblat |

# Emperor Napoléon's Family

**CHARLES MARIE BUONAPARTE**
(1746-1785)

married in 1764 to Letizia Ramolino
(Madame Mére)
(1749-1836)
8 children

## The Royal Line

As Emperor, Napoléon was generous to his family, bestowing titles and granting providence over a number of kingdoms. His desire to provide France with an heir would ultimately precipitate his divorce from his beloved Joséphine and marriage to the Austrian Archduchess Marie-Louise. In a twist of irony though, their son, the King of Rome (later the Duke of Reichstadt), would die young leaving no heir of his own. The children of Joséphine, on the other hand, would seat monarchs on the thrones of Europe. Hortense, in her marriage with Napoléon's brother Louis, would give birth to Napoléon III, Emperor of the French from 1851 to 1870. Eugène's daughter would marry the King of Sweden and Norway, and the lineage of their sons sits on numerous thrones to this day.

**JOSEPH**
(1768-1844)

King of Naples in 1806, King of Spain in 1808
married in 1794 Julie Clary

**NAPOLÉON I**
(1769-1821)

married in 1796 to Rose de Beauharnais
(the future Empress Joséphine)
married in 1810 to Marie-Louise, Archduchess of
Austria (the future Empress Marie-Louise)

**NAPOLEON II**
(1811-1832)

known as the King of Rome
and later the Duke of
Reichstadt

**LUCIEN**
(1775-1840)

1st Prince of Canino in 1815
married in 1794 to Christine Boyer
married in 1803 to Alexandrine Jacob de Bleschamp

**ELISA**
(1777-1820)

Princess of Piombino in 1805; and Lucca in 1806;
and Grand Dutchess of Tuscany in 1809
married in 1797 to Felix Bacciochi, Prince of Massa-
Carrara

**LOUIS**
(1778-1846)

King of Holland in 1806
married in 1802 to Hortense de Beauharnais,
Queen of Holland

**NAPOLEON CHARLES**
(1802-07)

**NAPOLEON LOUIS**
(1804-1831)

**LOUIS NAPOLEON**
(NAPOLEON III)
(1808-1873)

**PAULINE**
(1780-1825)

Princess Borghese and Dutchess of Guastalla
married Victor-Emmanuel Leclerc in 1797
married Prince Camille Borghese in 1803

**CAROLINE**
(1782-1839)

Grand Dutchess of Berg and Cleves in 1806, Queen
of Naples in 1808
married Joachim Murat in 1800
Grand Duke of Berg and Cleves, and King of Naples

**JÉRÔME**
(1784-1860)

King of Westphalia in 1807
married Elizabeth Patterson in 1803
married Princess Catherine de Württemberg in 1807

# Empress Joséphine's Descendents

**NAPOLÉON-CHARLES**
(1802-1807)

**HORTENSE DE BEAUHARNAIS**
(1783-1837)

Queen of Holland in 1806
married in 1802 to
Louis Bonaparte
(1778-1846)
King of Holland
3 children

**NAPOLÉON-LOUIS**
(1804-1831)

**LOUIS-NAPOLÉON**
(1808-1873)

future Napoléon III
Emperor of the French
(1851-1870)

**OSCAR**
(1861-1951)

Duke of Vastergoland

**OSCAR II**
(1829-1907)

King of Sweden
and Norway in 1872,
and King of Norway
only in 1905

**MARIE-JOSEPH-ROSE DE TASCHER DE LA PAGERIE**
(1763-1814)

Empress of France in 1804
married in 1779 to
Alexandre de Beauharnais
(1760-1794)
married in 1796 to
Napoléon Bonaparte
(1769-1821)

**EUGÈNE DE BEAUHARNAIS**
(1781-1824)

Prince of France and
Viceroy of Italy in 1805
married in 1806 to
Auguste-Amélie de
Baviere (1788-1851)
6 children

**JOSEPHINE DE LEUCHTENBERG**
(1807-1876)

married in 1823 to
Oscar I, King of Sweden
and Norway (1844)

**GUSTAVE V ADOLPHE**
(1858-1950)

King of Sweden in 1907

**CHARLES XV**
(1826-1872)

King of Sweden
and Norway (1859)

**LOUISE OF SWEDEN**
(1851-1926)

married in 1869 to
Frédéric VIII (1843-1912)
King of Denmark in 1906

Joséphine from the
*Book of Napoléon I's Coronation*

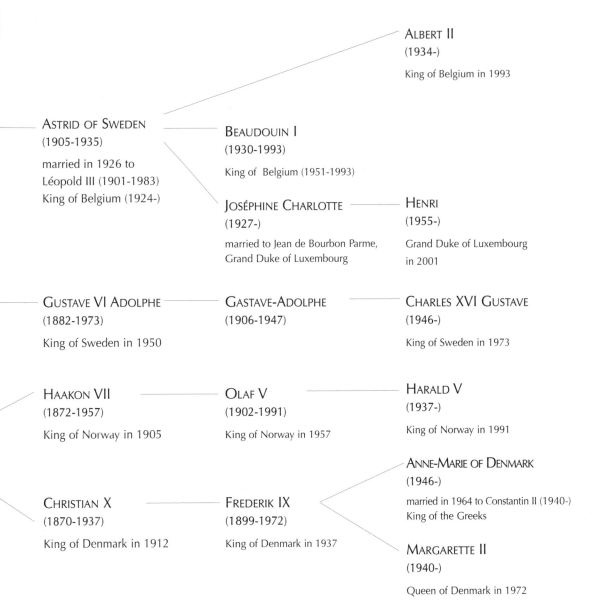

ALBERT II
(1934-)

King of Belgium in 1993

ASTRID OF SWEDEN
(1905-1935)

married in 1926 to
Léopold III (1901-1983)
King of Belgium (1924-)

BEAUDOUIN I
(1930-1993)

King of Belgium (1951-1993)

JOSÉPHINE CHARLOTTE
(1927-)

married to Jean de Bourbon Parme,
Grand Duke of Luxembourg

HENRI
(1955-)

Grand Duke of Luxembourg
in 2001

GUSTAVE VI ADOLPHE
(1882-1973)

King of Sweden in 1950

GASTAVE-ADOLPHE
(1906-1947)

CHARLES XVI GUSTAVE
(1946-)

King of Sweden in 1973

HAAKON VII
(1872-1957)

King of Norway in 1905

OLAF V
(1902-1991)

King of Norway in 1957

HARALD V
(1937-)

King of Norway in 1991

CHRISTIAN X
(1870-1937)

King of Denmark in 1912

FREDERIK IX
(1899-1972)

King of Denmark in 1937

ANNE-MARIE OF DENMARK
(1946-)

married in 1964 to Constantin II (1940-)
King of the Greeks

MARGARETTE II
(1940-)

Queen of Denmark in 1972

# A Napoleonic Era Timeline

**15 August 1769**
Napolione di Buonaparte born in Ajaccio, Corsica

**15 May 1779**
Napoléon (now using the French spelling) enters the Military College of Brienne in France

**17 October 1784**
Napoléon enters the Royal Military College of Paris and graduates 21 October 1785 as a Second Lieutenant

**1789–99**
The French Revolution

**1793**
The Siege of Toulon, where Napoléon is promoted to Brigadier General

**5 October 1795**
At the request of Director Barras, Napoléon crushes a royalist uprising, is promoted to General-in-Command - Army of the Interior and first meets Joséphine Beauharnais

**9 March 1796**
Napoléon marries Joséphine

**March 1796 – October 1797**
First Italian Campaigns, which include victories over the Austrians at Lodi, Arcola and Rivoli and the signing of the Treaty of Campo-Formio

**May 1798 – October 1799**
Egyptian Campaign, which ends with Napoléon's hasty return to Paris

**9-10 November 1799**
Napoléon seizes power in the Coup of 18 Brumaire, is elected First Consul of the Republic and declares the end of the Revolution

**May-June 1800**
Second Italian Campaign, where Napoléon defeats the Austrians on 14 June at the Battle of Marengo

**24 December 1800**
Napoléon survives bomb plot

**25 March 1802**
Treaty of Amiens signed with England

**4 August 1802**
Adoption of the new constitution and Napoléon made Consul for life

**3 May 1803**
Sale of the Louisiana Territory by France to the United States

**16 May 1803**
Peace of Amiens breaks down

**21 March 1804**
The Napoléonic Code established

**18 May 1804**
Napoléon proclaimed Emperor of the French and a new constitution creates an imperial monarchy

**2 December 1804**
Napoléon is crowned as Emperor by Pope Pius VII in Notre-Dame Cathedral

**17 May 1805**
Napoléon crowned King of Italy in the Milan Cathedral

**April-December 1805**
The Third Coalition of England, Naples, Russia and Austria formed against France, with Admiral Nelson destroying the French Fleet on 21 October at the Battle of Trafalgar

**2 December 1805**
Coalition dissolves with Napoléon's victory at the Battle of Austerlitz

**1 April 1806**
Napoléon's brother Joseph Bonaparte becomes King of Naples

**October 1806**
Fourth Coalition of England, Prussia and Russia formed against France but Napoléon gains victories at Jena and Auerstadt and enters Berlin on 27 October

**21 November 1806**
The Continental Blockade begins, closing continental ports to British ships

**14 June 1807**
The Russians are defeated at Friedland and the Treaty of Tilsit is signed between Czar Alexander I of Russia and Napoléon on 7 July

**22 July 1807**
Grand Duchy of Warsaw created

**16 August 1807**
Napoléon's brother Jerome becomes King of Westphalia

**30 November 1807**
The French occupy Portugal and seize Lisbon on 1 December

**20 February 1808**
Occupation of Spain begins under the command of Murat and Joseph becomes King of Spain on 4 June (Murat replaces him in Naples)

**April-October 1809**
Napoléon defeats Austria on 5 July at the Battle of Wagram and then enters Vienna

**15 December 1809**
Napoléon divorces Joséphine in order to remarry and conceive an heir

**2 April 1810**
Napoléon marries Archduchess Marie-Louise of Austria in religious ceremony

**31 December 1810**
Russia breaks with Napoléon

**20 March 1811**
Napoléon and Marie-Louise's son, the King of Rome, is born

**19 June 1812**
United States declares war with Britain

**June-December 1812**
The Russian campaign, where Napoléon is forced, for the first time, to retreat and the Grand Army is decimated

**March-November 1813**
Sixth Coalition of England, Austria, Prussia and Russia formed against France, with Wellington taking Madrid on 12 August, victory at Leipzig on 15 October in the Battle of Nations, Napoléonic Germany collapsing and Holland being lost

**January-March 1814**
Allied troops enter France with the fall of Paris on 30-31 March

**4 April 1814**
Napoléon abdicates unconditionally at Fontainebleau, royal authority under the Bourbons is re-established, returning France to a constitutional monarchy, and Empress Marie-Louise and the King of Rome flee to Bois

**4 May 1814**
Napoléon exiled to the island of Elba off the coast of Italy where he is made ruler and retains his title as Emperor

**29 May 1814**
Empress Joséphine dies at the Château of Malmaison

**March-June 1815**
Napoléon escapes from Elba and lands at Golfe Juan in the south of France, his old armies rally to his side as he marches to Paris, Louis XVIII flees to Ghent on 20 March and Napoléon reigns again for what is known as "The Hundred Days"

**18 June 1815**
Wellington and Blücher defeat Napoléon at the Battle of Waterloo

**22 June 1815**
Napoléon's second abdication at the Elysée Palace in Paris which is followed by his surrender to the English on 15 July

**17 October 1815**
Napoléon is exiled to St. Helena, a barren island in the South Atlantic

**15 April 1821**
Napoléon dies in his home, Longwood, on St. Helena

**22 July 1832**
Napoléon's son, the King of Rome, who became the Duke of Reichstadt in 1816, dies

**May-December 1840**
The English Government allows the Emperor's ashes to be returned to France, his body is exhumed on 15 October and placed in the Invalides in Paris on 15 December

**17 December 1847**
Empress Marie-Louise, who was made the reigning Duchess of Parma in 1815 by the Congress of Vienna, dies

**15 December 1940**
Adolph Hitler returns the ashes of Napoléon's son to Paris for internment in the Invalides

# The Rise to Power

**B**orn on the island of Corsica off the western coast of Italy into a family of minor nobility, Napoléon gained admission to France's Brienne military school as Corsica had become a provence of France just before his birth. Arriving at the school at the tender age of 9, he found himself friendless and ostracized because of his relative poverty and thick Italian accent. He read incessantly and excelled in math and geography. At 16, he was commissioned as a second lieutenant in the artillery. His genius as an artillery officer led to early military successes. The first was at the siege of Toulon, where his strategy forced the British fleet to retire.  Later in Paris, he used his artillery regiment to disperse a crowd that threatened the ruling Directory. Paul Barras, the Directory's head, repaid Napoléon for his help by putting him in charge of the Army of Italy. Barras also introduced the young general to the widow Rose de Beauharnais. Napoléon married this sophisticated, yet kind beauty and gave her a new name – Joséphine.

*"Bonaparte at the Arcole Bridge"*
After Baron Antoine-Jean Gros — 1798
Napoléon crossed a bridge under enemy fire at the head of his men to help win the battle of Arcole, one of the most significant of his First Italian Campaign. Gros' famous painting of the young commander became an icon of his military mastery.
Lithograph engraving. First print.

## "General Bonaparte Commanding the Army of Italy in 1797"

Andrea Appiani, engraved by Alix — c. 1797

The is the first known portrait of Napoléon. It captures the courage and decisiveness of the 28-year-old general, who during the first Italian campaign, defeated three opposing armies with forces outnumbered two to one.

Engraving

## Mathematics book belonging to Napoléon at Brienne

M. Bossut, author — 1781

This is the earliest known book from Napoléon's school days. He had a passion for books. Visiting Paris for the first time after military school, his first purchase was a book, *Gil Blas,* the story of an impoverished but adventurous Spanish boy who becomes successful.

Leatherbound book

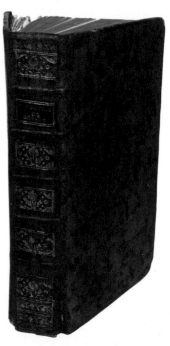

## Letter written by Napoléon Bonaparte at age 14
1784

Writing to his cousin Arigo di Casaneuva from military school in Paris, Napoléon details his day-to-day schedule, showing his organizational skills as well as his command of French, which was not his first language. Still using the original Italian spelling of his name, which he would later convert to the French form, he signs the letter "Napolione di Buonaparte."

Ink on paper

### Leather portfolio used by Paul Barras at the National Convention, 1792-95

Paul Barras was a founding member of the five-member "Directory" entrusted in the new constitution of 1795 with the executive power. He was also the most important political figure of Napoléon's early career, making him a full general in command of the Army of Italy at 26. Barras also introduced his protégé to the Creole beauty Marie-Josèphe-Rose de Beauharnais, soon to be known forevermore as Joséphine.

Gilt-tooled red Morocco leather with silver clasp

### "Crossing the Bridge at Lodi"

Engraving after Carle Vernet — c. 1806

At Lodi, during the First Italian Campaign, facing heavy fire from Austrian guns on the far bank, Napoléon decided to storm the river's wooden bridge. Astride a white horse, he road up and down the ranks, working his troops' courage up to a fever pitch. With the drum and fifes playing *La Marseillaise*, he gave the order and the French forces charged, shouting, "Vive la République!" By the end of the day, victory was theirs. This day was a psychological turning point for Napoléon, who became truly aware of his extraordinary powers of leadership.

# The Egyptian Campaign

I n 1798, Napoléon convinced the Directory to authorize the bold plan of invading Egypt to block British trade routes and divert English military energy from attacking France. The campaign began well but ended in calamity. First, British Admiral Nelson destroyed the French fleet at Aboukir. This trapped the already beleaguered French troops in the Middle East, ultimately causing over 50% casualties due to disease and combat. Learning of the deteriorating political situation in France, Napoléon secretly set sail for France to rescue a government in disarray and perhaps gain further status for himself. He handed over his Egyptian command to the capable General Jean-Baptiste Kléber, who was furious at being left in an impossible situation. Though clearly not a military success, the Egyptian campaign was to have a long-lasting impact. The team of artists, scientists and writers that Napoléon took with him to the Middle East were the first westerners to catalogue the wonders of the historic region. Their work sparked a fascination with ancient Egypt that has continued to this day.

"General Bonaparte Commanding the Army of Italy"
Andrea Appiani. Engraving by Alix — 1798
One of the first known engravings of General Bonaparte, it captures the resolution and intensity that produced the extraordinary successes of the First Italian Campaign from March 1796 to December 1797.
Historical Provenance — Contesse de Chambure collection
Engraving with watercolor

### "Bonaparte on Horseback in Cairo with His Staff"

Nicolas-Toussaint Charlet --- c. 1820

Patterning himself after Alexander the Great, Napoléon invited well-known scholars, scientists and artists to accompany the army to Egypt in May 1798. They would document all they found for three years. The scholars' or savants' (as they were known) investigation of the *"Rosetta Stone,"* first discovered in 1799 by French soldiers building a fort at Rosetta near Rashid, would ultimately lead to the modern decipherment of Egyptian heiroglyphics.

Historical Provenance --- the collection of Charles-Roux

Watercolor and gouache

### "Portrait of General Jean-Baptiste Kléber"

Baron Pierre-Narcisse Guérin --- 1798

After 14 months in Egypt, Napoléon returned to France in August 1799, one of several times he appeared to abandon his men when victory became unlikely. He appointed the courageous General Jean-Baptiste Kléber to take charge of the doomed Egyptian expedition, which was to cost France nearly 40,000 soldiers.

Historical Provenance --- The Bonaparte family collection

Miniature on ivory

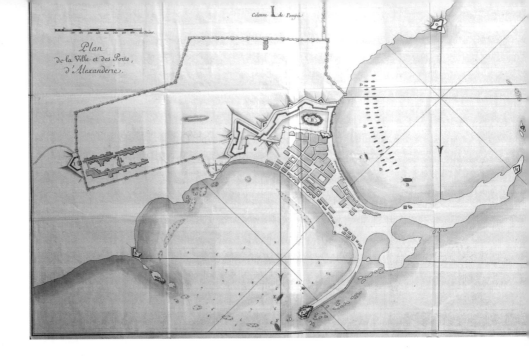

## Map of the city and harbors of Alexandria

1798

Painted by cartographers attached to the expedition, this map shows the disposition of the French fleet at Alexandria in July 1798, when Napoléon landed there.

Watercolor on paper

## "The School of Fine Arts"

Jean-Baptiste Kléber — 1780

This drawing of the School of Fine Arts was executed by Jean-Baptiste Kléber in 1780, when he was a student in the school. He was an architect in Strasbourg before joining the army in 1783. Kléber later became one of Napoléon's generals, playing an instrumental role in the expedition to Egypt.

Graphite with watercolor

## Sketch for "Battle of the Pyramids"

François-André Vincent —— c. 1800

In this French victory, the brave, though lightly armed Mamelukes were no match for the heavy guns of the French forces, formed here in squares. Overwhelmed, the Egyptian infantry panicked, scattered and tried to escape by swimming the Nile. Always the student of history, Napoléon preceeded the military engagement by telling his troops, "Soldiers, from the height of these pyramids forty centuries look down upon you."

Historical Provenance —— Ordered by Napoléon for Marshal Louis Berthier

Ink and sepia wash

## Eugène de Beauharnais' first promotion

Signed by Alexandre Berthier —— 1798

This is the official document promoting Joséphine's son, Eugène de Beauharnais, to Lieutenant and Aide de Camp to Napoléon. It is signed by General Louis Alexandre Berthier, Napoléon's chief of staff, in Cairo. This is the Eugène's first promotion. He was to become Viceroy of Italy and regularly fight at his stepfather's side.

## "The Ray" from "Description of Egypt"

Annotations by Pierre Joseph Redouté, intended for naturalist Geoffroy de Saint-Hilaire

The artist has marked this proof prior to its finalization as a plate for engraving. Both Redouté and Saint-Hilaire formed part of Napoléon's scientific corps in Egypt. Saint-Hilaire went on to become a general, fighting at Austerlitz, Eylau, and other decisive battles.

Engraving with ink

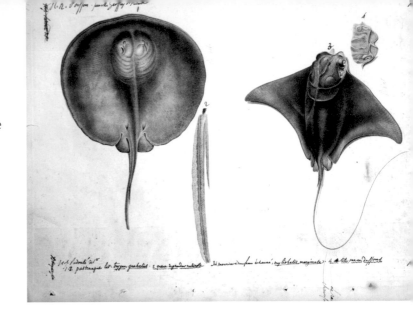

## Engravings from "Description of Egypt"

c. 1809

The *Description of Egypt* was published in eleven sumptuous, beautifully illustrated folio volumes following the return of the French army in 1801. They included all the research and observations made by the scientific corps that had accompanied the army. The publication of these volumes would spark the birth of the science of Egyptology.

Engraving on paper

# First Consul

**W**hen Napoléon returned to Paris from Egypt on October 16, 1799, his clever self-promotional campaign was a success and he was greeted as a hero. On the 18th Brumaire (November 9), he seized power over the French government in a bloodless coup and became First Consul. The other two consuls, Jean Jacques Cambacérès and Charles Francois Lebrun, were silent partners in the government. Consolidating power in his own hands, Napoléon took measures to institutionalize the gains of the French Revolution. He quickly began a series of sweeping initiatives that restored political stability to the country. He reformed and revitalized the legal system through the Napoleonic Code. As a means of encouraging individual contributions to the French nation, Napoléon instituted the order of the Legion of Honour in 1802. He also patronized the arts, encouraged manufacturing and started building public works, sparking economic and architectural development that changed the face of France and of Europe itself.

*"First Consul Bonaparte"*
Baron Antoine-Jean Gros — c. 1802
As First Consul, Napoléon distinguished himself from the other two, Jean Jacques Cambacérès and Charles François Lebrun, by dressing in red, while they dressed in blue. Napoléon commissioned Gros to paint his official portrait as First Consul, as well as a series of copies intended as gifts for friends or to be sent to specific towns to commemorate his latest successes. Only a handful of these copies remain, most being destroyed during the political upheavals following Napoléon's period in power.

Gros was introduced to Bonaparte by Joséphine, and Napoléon admired the artist greatly. The young and ambitious Consul was famous for his lack of willingness to sit for portraits, and he was too impatient or busy to sit for this work. Gros was consequently forced to use studies he had made for "Bonaparte at the Bridge of Arcole," hence the similarity to that portrait.
Historical Provenance — Commissioned by Napoléon
Oil on canvas

## Study for "18th Brumaire"

Francoise Bouçhot — c. 1840

This study for a illustrative series commissioned by King Louis-Philippe, shows Napoléon in the Council of Five Hundred on November 10, 1799. The Council, presided over by his brother Lucien, was meeting in St. Cloud, a suburb of Paris. At this stage it was unclear whether Napoléon's attempt to take over the government would succeed.

Historical Provenance — Pierre Miquel collection

Sepia ink and sepia on paper

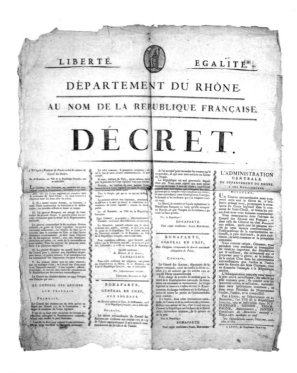

## Printed decree of the French Republic announcing the "Coup d'Etat of the 18th Brumaire"

November 1799

This decree announces the decisions taken by the Council of Five Hundred following the 18th Brumaire (November 9, 1799) and the first decisions made by General Napoléon Bonaparte when he was still the general in command of the Paris garrison.

Printing on paper

## Petition to the Minister of the Interior

1799

Napoléon actively supported the arts and appreciated the art of engraving, commissioning numerous engraved depictions of his military campaigns. Here the great artists of the era, including Jacques-Louis David, François Gérard, Honoré Fragonard, Charles Percier, Pierre François Léonard Fontaine and Pierre Redouté request that the French state officially recognize the value of engraving.

Ink on paper

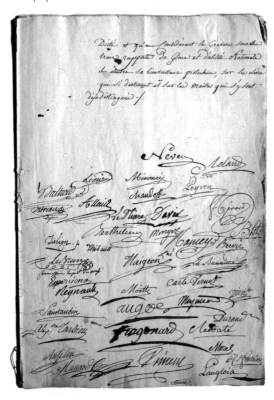

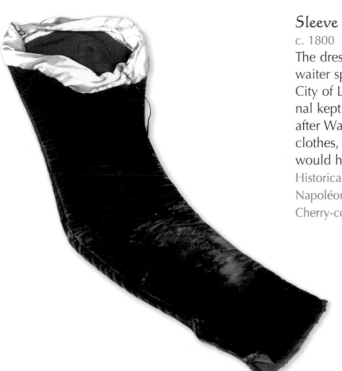

## Sleeve of the dress coat of First Consul Bonaparte
c. 1800

The dress coat from which this sleeve was removed, after a waiter spilled sauce on it, was a gift to Napoléon from the City of Lyon. The family of the tailor who replaced the original kept the damaged sleeve. The rest of this coat was lost after Waterloo. Napoléon was notoriously frugal about clothes, often repairing pants, coats and shoes that others would have simply replaced.

Historical Provenance — The family of M. Le Chevalier, Napoléon's tailor
Cherry-colored Naccara silk velvet

## "Bonaparte Visiting the Silk Manufacturers of Rouen"
Jean-Baptiste Isabey — 1802

Passionate about encouraging French industry, Napoléon frequently visited factories, showing an interest in their products and manufacturing techniques, giving prizes and purchasing goods for his palaces. Here he is introduced to an old man who worked in the factory with indefatigable zeal for 53 years. The Consul would reward the man with an annual pension of 400 Francs.

Historical Provenance — Prince Joachim Murat collection
India ink and sepia on paper

## Bust of Napoléon

Jean-Antoine Houdon --- c. 1804

This sculpture shows Napoléon in the latter period of his Consular period. Napoléon seldom sat for portraits, but did for the original from which this studio mold this was cast.

Plaster on a marble base

## Grand Eagle Legion of Honour Medallion of Emperor Napoléon Bonaparte

after 1802

To recognize the talent and achievement of men from all fields, Napoléon established the Legion of Honour in 1802, its name reprising the glory of the Roman republic. The Legion included members, officers, commanders and grand officers, organized into cohorts. The Grand Eagle was the highest award. Napoléon wore this medallion on the left breast of his uniforms.

Historical Provenance --- Lucien Bonaparte family collection

Silver thread on fabric

## Snuffbox of First Consul Napoléon Bonaparte

Silversmith by the name of Marguerite --- c. 1800-02

Napoléon was an active man who constantly fiddled with personal possessions. One can imagine him taking this box for tobacco powder out of his pocket and stroking it during meetings with his ministers. His principal antidotes to stress were inhaling pinches of snuff and sucking on anise flavored liquorice. This box was probably a present from Joséphine.

Historical Provenance --- Josèphine Bonaparte family through Prince Eugène

Gold and enamel

## Gold medal awarded to Firmin Didot by First Consul Napoléon Bonaparte

1800

Napoléon awarded this medal to the publisher Firmin Didot during the first industrial exhibition he sponsored to encourage French manufacturing, held at the Louvre in 1801. The medal represents a character with Phrygian cap (France) surrounded with different symbols: a plow for agriculture; a paddle for navigation; a compass for industry; and a caduceus for trade. It is engraved with the words "Encouragement and reward to the industry."

Historical Provenance --- Firmin Didot family collection

22-carat gold

### Minister of Treasury Barbé Marbois Portfolio, which carried the Louisiana Treaty of Sale in 1803
c. 1800-03

Napoléon had gained control of the Louisiana Territory from Spain in 1800 as part of an effort to create a new empire centered on the Caribbean sugar trade, as well as a base from which to challenge the British in the Caribbean. The strategy did not succeed, and he decided to sell the 800,000 square miles of land, which extended from the Mississippi River to the Rocky Mountains, to the United States for about $15 million.

Historical Provenance ---- Barbé Marbois family collection
Green Morocco leather with gilding

### "Apotheosis of Napoléon Bonaparte, First Consul of the Republic"
Constance Meyer and Pierre-Paul Prudhon ---- 1803

Napoléon understood the value of controlling his image and using the arts to instill respect and admiration for himself and his policies. As if a conquering Roman general, the Consul stands on a chariot with a laurel crown on his head, symbolizing the passage from the Republic to the Empire era. The young women's items represent both victory and death, joy and sorrow.

Oil on canvas

# The Coronation

O n December 2, 1804, Napoléon and Joséphine were crowned Emperor and Empress of the French by Pope Pius VII in a ceremony in Notre-Dame Cathedral. One purpose of this move was to legitimize his government. He also wished to elevate himself to the same level as other European sovereigns. The title of Emperor reflected his and his nation's esteem for the Roman Republic, as well as France's growth in size through the wars that had created an empire across Europe. The coronation featured lavish decorative elements, elaborate fashions, and imposing architectural facades constructed within the cathedral and across Paris. To make the event as impressive as possible, Napoléon enlisted exceptional artists, including Jean-Baptiste Isabey, Jacques-Louis David, and designers Charles Percier and Pierre François Léonard Fontaine.

*"Portrait of Napoléon I in Coronation Robe"*
Baron François Gérard — c. 1805-10
In December 1804, Napoléon had himself crowned Emperor to create a dynasty, protect the French Republic, and place himself on a par with other European sovereigns. The lavish coronation ceremony was planned as carefully as a military campaign. Gérard's portrait records the 35-year-old ruler's supreme confidence. It also illustrates the symbolism of the occasion, seen in such features as the laurel crown on Napoléon's head, reminiscent of a Roman emperor, and the elaborate necklace of eagles, the imperial emblem, adorning his chest. The Emperor gave this portrait to Talleyrand, his devious Minister of Foreign Affairs.
Historical Provenance — Valençay Castle collection
Oil on canvas. Gold frame sculpted by Ménan

## "Central Nave of Notre-Dame Cathedral" from the "Book of the Coronation"

Charles Percier and Pierre François Léonard Fontaine —— 1807

Completed after nearly two centuries in 1345, Notre-Dame has stood at the heart of French history for hundreds of years. In 1793, with the closure of many of the French churches, the cathedral was vandalized and looted. For nearly a decade, it was used as a warehouse for food. Napoléon restored religious freedoms in 1802. The coronation at Notre-Dame two years later elevated this powerful symbol of the country to its rightful place once again.

Historical Provenance —— Talleyrand collection
Engraving and watercolor

## "The Imperial Procession Entering Notre-Dame Cathedral" from the "Book of the Coronation"

Charles Percier and Pierre François Léonard Fontaine —— 1807

With a large coronation party and 8,000 dignitaries in attendance, protocol was of primary concern. Napoléon's family caused a number of problems, with two of his sisters refusing to carry Joséphine's train because it was beneath their status as "Highnesses," which Napoléon had just conferred. Exasperated, he remarked, "One would think, to hear you, that I had just despoiled you of the heritage of our late father the king."

Historical Provenance —— Talleyrand collection
Engraving and watercolor

## Pope Pius VII and clergymen

Claude-Louis Desrais — c. 1805

In this study, the Pope and clergy are seen as they were during a moment in the coronation processional.

Indian ink and gouache

## Portrait of Pope Pius VII

Auguste GarnerayProvenance — 1805

Pope Pius VII agreed to crown Napoléon because he had already gained concessions for the church in the Concordant of 1801, which reestablished Catholicism as the religion of France, and assumed that, as Emperor, Napoléon would further reward the church. This did not happen, and in July 1809, Napoléon's officers arrested Pius VII when he refused to resign as Pope and Head of the Papal States.

Engraving embellished with watercolors

## Preparatory study for the Imperial eagle

Antoine Denis Chaudet --- 1804

At Napoléon's coronation, the single-headed eagle became the symbol of the French Empire, helping to brand his sovereignty. The eagle was the symbol of Imperial Rome and has been associated with military victory since antiquity. This was a design for one of the Emperor's carriages.

Crayon on paper

## "The Coronation"

Charles Percier and Pierre François Léonard Fontaine, after Jacques-Louis David --- c. 1807-1808

Having placed the crown on his own head, as previously agreed with Pope Pius VII, Napoléon next placed a crown on Joséphine's head, who was moved to tears by the gesture. For him, this was the highlight of the coronation. When he saw David's rendition of the ceremony, from which this drawing is taken, he said "Well done, David. You have guessed what I had in mind... you have shown me as a French knight."

Watercolor and gouache on paper

## "Napoléon I in Coronation Robe"

Gobelins, after François Gérard --- 1812

For his coronation, Napoléon wore a purple velvet cloak, lined with ermine and embroidered with bees. His crown was gold laurel leaves, intended to recall the glory of the Roman Republic. All of his life, he was conscious of symbolism and iconography. This oval tapestry was made after Gérard's official painting. In total, nine copies were executed: eight busts and one full size. Louis XVIII ordered all of them destroyed, and only three survived: one in New York's Metropolitan Museum of Art; one in a private collection; and the one in this exhibition.

Historical Provenance --- Prince Murat family collection

Tapestry

## Sword of the Chief of Heralds, used to proclaim Napoléon emperor

Designed by Jacques-Louis David and Jean Baptist Isabey. Manufactured by Nicolas Noel Boutet at the Versailles imperial armory. --- 1804

During the three-hour coronation ceremony, the Imperial couple sat on their thrones, which were placed on a platform under Notre Dame Cathedral's main arch. The enthronement conferred on Napoléon the supreme power of France. It fell to the Chief of the Heralds to proclaim him Emperor and announce the coronation to the crowd.

Historical Provenance --- Charles Marchal collection

Gilded bronze, silver-gilt, ebony, and velvet.

## Cushion used at coronation of Napoléon

1804

Many of the objects used in the coronation displayed Napoléon's personal emblem, the bee. The symbol provided continuity with Charlemagne, King of the Franks and Holy Roman Emperor, who had used the bee as his personal emblem a thousand years before. Ancient Egyptians, Romans and Christians all associated the bee and the hive with industry and regeneration, wisdom and obedience. The bee also appears in the symbology of the Freemasons, of which Napoléon was one.

Historical Provenance — Collection of Augustin François André Picot, the Emperor's embroiderer
Silk velvet, gold thread and embroidered braid

## Foot cushion used at coronation of Napoléon

c. 1804

These elaborate, gold-embroidered cushions were used by the high-ranking ecclesiastical dignitaries.

Historical Provenance — Collection of Augustin François André Picot, the Emperor's embroiderer
Red velvet with embroidery

## Fragment of wall covering which decorated Notre-Dame Cathedral for coronation

Brocard  1804

Brocard was responsible for the production of all textiles used for the coronation.

Historical Provenance — Collection of Augustin François André Picot, the Emperor's embroiderer
Red velvet with gold embroidery

Ceremonial dress coat of a
senior member of the Council
of State
1804
Jean-Pierre Baghasson, Comte de
Montalivet, Napoléon's Minister of
the Interior, wore this dress coat at
the coronation.
Historical Provenance ---
De Montalivet family collection
Silk velvet and silk embroidery

## Large wooden plaque used at the coronation

Designed by Jacques-Louis David. Manufactured by Jacob —– 1804

Of the 10 coats of arms designed as supporting accents for the red velvet that surrounded the nave of Notre-Dame Cathedral, only one remains. Surrounding the Imperial Eagle is the Collier (ceremonial necklace) of the Legion of Honour. Modeled after those used by Charlemagne, the staff on the left portrays the hand of justice giving a benediction and the scepter on the right portrays Charlemagne, the first emperor of the west, on his throne. At the top is the crown of the Empire and below it is drapery embroidered with bees.

Historical Provenance —– Charles Marchal collection

Fruitwood

## "Apotheosis of Napoléon"

Charles Meynier — c. 1809

This was the study for an engraving ordered by Napoléon to celebrate the first five years of the Empire and its many achievements. The large, single sheet of paper on which it was drawn was specially manufactured for the piece, and its size is unusual for the period.

Historical Provenance — From the Marshal Soult's collection

Ink and graphite on paper

## Gold medal commemorating Emperor Napoléon I's coronation

Andrieu foundry — 1804

In this medal, intended for one of his family members, Napoléon looks every bit the Roman emperor.

Historical Provenance — Marshall Louis Alexandre Berthier family collection

Gold

## "Napoléon Wearing the Coronation Regalia of the King of Italy"

Jean-Baptiste Isabey Provenance — December 1852

Six months after the coronation in Paris, the Emperor was crowned "King of Italy" in Milan. Isabey executed this drawing in December 1852, at the time of Napoléon III's coup d'etat. Napoléon III was the son of Joséphine's daughter, Queen Hortense of Holland, and of Napoléon's brother, Louis, the King of Holland. This birth of the "Second Empire" in France provided inspiration for the artist's sentimental *souvenir* (remembrance) of the First Empire.

Historical Provenance — Prince Napoléon Murat collection

Graphite on paper

## Sketch of Eugène de Beauharnais' sabretache for the Emperor's coronation

Carle Vernet — 1804

This drawing shows the power of the Imperial emblem Napoléon selected for his coronation—the single-headed eagle. Other contenders were the cock, the lion and the elephant.

Historical Provenance — Picot collection

Watercolor and gouache on paper

# The Emperor's Family

The second of eight children, Napoléon was close to his mother and siblings, who played a key role in his life and in the governance of his vast Empire. His brothers and sisters received royal titles and frequently were entrusted with regions of the Empire to rule, though none were to match his genius as an administrator. Napoléon was intensely loyal. His beloved first wife, Joséphine, and her two children, Eugène and Hortense de Beauharnais, forever shared a place in his heart, even after he divorced Joséphine in 1809 after nearly 14 years of marriage which unfortunately, had not produced him an heir. His second wife, the Austrian Archduchess Marie-Louise, quickly gave him a son he adored, born in 1811, whom he crowned the King of Rome.

**"Prince Eugène de Beauharnais"**
Queen Hortense de Beauharnais and Baron Antoine-Jean Gros
— c. 1800
One of the earliest representations of Eugène, it depicts him at age 18 as Napoléon's aide-de-camp in the Egyptian campaign. Napoléon was close to both of his stepchildren. He adopted Eugène in 1805, and then made him a prince and later Viceroy of Italy. Though Hortense was a talented artist, it is Gros' genius at portraiture that shines through here.
Historical Provenance — Joséphine Bonaparte family collection
Oil on canvas

## Pauline Borghèse's snuffbox

c. 1808-1810

Pauline, Napoléon's favorite sister, demonstrated undying loyalty to her brother. She was beautiful, seductive and had many lovers. She gave this snuffbox to her sister, Caroline Murat.

Gold and tortoise shell

## Strongbox of King Joseph of Spain

Martin-Guillaume Biennais — c. 1810

Napoléon and his older brother, Joseph, were rivals as children. As an adult, Joseph bridled at taking orders from his younger brother, although the Emperor conferred both honors and responsibilities on him, including making him King of Naples and later King of Spain. This safe was captured by the English at the Battle of Vittoria in June 1813.

Historical Provenance — Duke of Wellington family collection

Mahogony, ebony, bronze and silver

## Prince Joachim Murat's inkwell with clock

Clock movement by Bréguet — 1805

Napoléon gave this elaborate inkwell in the shape of a ship with Poseidon standing in the center to his brother-in-law Joachim Murat when he appointed him Prince and Grand Admiral of the Empire. One of the great cavalry officers of the 19th century, Murat would ultimately be named King of Naples after Joseph became King of Spain.

Historical Provenance — Murat Family collection

## "Caroline Murat"

Louis Lafittec — 1809

One of Napoléon's least favorite and most ambitious siblings, Caroline married Joachim Murat and became queen of Naples. When the Emperor's fortunes turned, Caroline and her husband conspired against him to remain in power.

Historical Provenance — Commissioned by Napoléon for the French Senate at Luxembourg Palace.

Graphite and gouache on paper

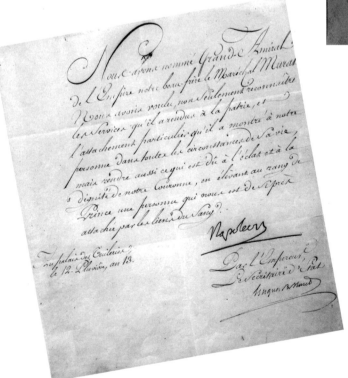

## Murat's appointment as Prince and Grand Admiral of the Empire

1807

In 1807, Napoléon began to create an Imperial Nobility. Through the end of his reign he was to name 31 dukes, 452 counts, 1,500 barons and 1,474 chevaliers. Among them, his brother-in-law Joachim Murat, a superb cavalry officer, was surprised to be made Grand Admiral of the Empire.

Ink on paper

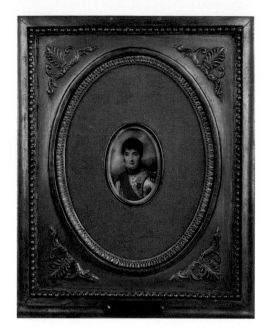

## "Jérôme Bonaparte, King of Westphalia"

Jean-Baptiste Isabey --- 1810

The youngest of the Bonaparte family, Jérôme was often a source of frustration and disappointment to Napoléon. In 1803, he married Elizabeth Patterson of Baltimore, Maryland, without his brother's consent. Napoléon's response was to annul the marriage, force him to wed Princess Catherine of Württemberg and make him King of Westphalia.

Historical Provenance --- Comte Simeon collection
Ivory, gold and blue enamel

## Design for standard of King Jérôme of Westphalia's Bodyguards

Carle Verne

Meant to be embroidered, this is a study for the standard of the 3rd squadron of Jérôme's bodyguards.

Historical Provenance --- Picot Collection
Watercolor on paper

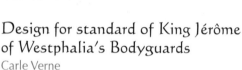

## Imperial bed of Jérôme Bonaparte, King of Westphalia (detail)

Jacob --- c. 1810

Jérôme was known for his taste for luxury, and this bed, from the palace at Kassel, attests to his penchant for splendor. It celebrates Napoléon's military conquests with Egyptian figures and stars, and honors his victories with oak and laurel branches.

The bed's fabric has been recreated by the House of Prelle, which was established in Lyon in 1752 and furnished the Emperor's palaces. Using their authentic Empire designs, Prelle often utilizes its original period looms to create its silk and brocades. This is the only royal bed of the First Empire in a private collection.

Historical Provenance --- Duc de Montebello family collection

## First Consul Bonaparte standing in front of Malmaison

Jean-Baptiste Isabey — 1802

Napoléon is depicted here, perhaps for the first time, in a characteristic pose that would become his signature stance. Joséphine purchased Malmaison early in their marriage, and spent lavish amounts of money making it a beautiful and comfortable residence. It was a place where Napoléon could truly relax.

Historical Provenance — Joachim Murat's collection

Engraving

## Items from Napoléon and Joséphine's Sèvres porcelain service

Manufacture Imperiale de Sèvres — c. 1804

This service was presented to Napoléon and Joséphine by the Sèvres company on January 1, 1805, following the coronation. The pattern reflects the neoclassical style of the Empire period.

Porcelain

## Joséphine's monogrammed tortoise shell box
c. 1799-1800

The opposite of Napoléon in temperament, Joséphine loved to spend money on beautiful objects. He gave her a monthly allowance of 50,000 francs for personal expenses and 10,000 for charities, but her spending often exceeded that.

Historical Provenance ---- Marshal Ney's collection
Tortoise shell ornamented with guilloche

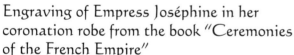

## Engraving of Empress Joséphine in her coronation robe from the book "Ceremonies of the French Empire"
1805

On the day of her ascension to the throne, Joséphine shimmered with diamonds, wearing a gown of white satin and mantle made of gold-embroidered velvet. Although not a great beauty, she had pretty chestnut hair, dark blue eyes, long lashes and a sexy, languid style. Napoléon said of her, "Truly she was more full of grace than any woman I have ever seen."

Historical Provenance ---- Emperor's library in Compiègne
Engraving

## Joséphine's books from Malmaison

Given little early schooling, Joséphine could barely read until she was a young adult. After learning, she developed a passion for books. The library at Malmaison covered a broad range of topics, showing the Imperial couple's interests and intellect. With her prayer book, bound in red Morocco leather, is a volume from *Delandine's New Historical Dictionary 1804,* evidencing the love of history she shared with her husband.

Historical Provenance ---- Library of Malmaison
Leather and paper

## Embroidery of roses given by City of Lyon to Joséphine

c. 1808

Joséphine was inordinately fond of roses, cultivating them at Malmaison. In fact, many varieties that are popular today originated in her gardens. She also commissioned nature artist Pierre Joseph Redouté to paint her roses.

Silk thread

## Joséphine's portfolio for the annulment papers

This artifact is one of two almost identical portfolios, which originally contained the official documents annulling Napoléon and Joséphine's marriage, along with affidavits testifying to the irregularity of their religious marriage.

Red Morocco leather

## Lock of Empress Joséphine's hair

This lock of Joséphine's hair was collected by her private physician, Dr. Lamoureux, on the day of her death, May 29, 1814.

Historical Provenance — Prince Murat collection

Human hair in cloth ribbon

### Engraved portrait of Eugène de Beauharnais

Engraved with watercolors by
Alix — c. 1805
Prince Eugene was
Joséphine's only son, whom
Napoléon made Viceroy of
Italy. He is seen here in his
official uniform. From the
first time Napoléon met
him, he was impressed by
the young man's modesty,
sincerity and good looks.
Engraving embellished with
watercolors

### "Troubadour Scene"

Queen Hortense — c. 1808-1810
Joséphine's daughter was a talented woman, interested in
the arts and literature. Here, she painted an historical
scene of a château in the Loire Valley.
Historical Provenance — Madame d'Arjuson collection
India ink drawing

### Snuffbox belonging to Queen Hortense

Vachette
At Napoléon's request, Hortense
married his brother Louis Bonaparte, and the two became king and
queen of Holland. Although they
had three sons (one of them the
future Napoléon III), the marriage
was unhappy and they separated in
1810. Hortense always remained
supportive of her stepfather, which
led to her banishment from France
after his final defeat.
Gold box in red Morocco leather case

## Birth certficate of Charles Napoléon

October 1804

Charles was the son of Queen Hortense and Louis Bonaparte. The birth certificate is signed by Napoléon, Joséphine, Napoléon's brother Joseph and his wife Julie. Signed just prior to the coronation, it is one of the few documents in existence with both the future Emperor and Empress' signatures together.

Ink on paper

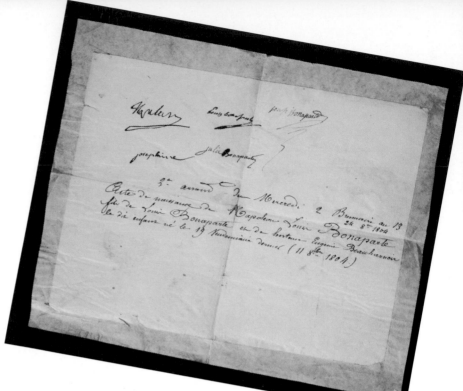

## Teapot given by Empress Marie-Louise to Queen Hortense

Manufacture Imperiale de Sèvres --- 1813

The teapot's decorative motifs were taken from artwork by Charles Percier and Pierre François Léonard Fontaine, inspired by the 17th-century fables of Jean La Fontaine representing two friends.

Historical Provenance --- Bonaparte family collection

## Napoléon's signet ring

Etienne Nitot (today: Chaumet) --- c. 1809

This is the only remaining example of ten similar rings commissioned by Napoléon. The Emperor gave this one to the Commander of his Honor Guard, Hans de Bruyère of Nimegue, during his honeymoon with Marie-Louise in September 1810.

Historical Provenance --- Commander Hans de Bruyere family collection.

10.5 Carat of diamonds with additional brilliants in gold

## Busts of Empress Marie-Louise and Napoléon I

Manufacture Imperiale de Sèvres after François Joseph Bosio; laurels by Thomire --- 1811

These busts in the classical style were intended as personal or diplomatic presents from the Emperor and Empress. The pairs were made in different sizes. Most were broken when the kings returned to the French throne, and today only two sets remain of both Napoléon and Marie-Louise.

Bisque on marble base with gilded bronze

◀

## "Empress Marie-Louise"
Baron François Gérard

Marie-Louise of Austria, the oldest of seven, was the daughter of François II, Emperor of Austria. She was fluent in French and cultivated in art and music. At the age of 40, Napoléon, for political reasons and anxious to found a dynasty, married the eighteen year old Marie-Louise. They grew very attached to each other and Napoléon covered her with jewels. On March 20, 1811, the King of Rome was born. After the fall of the Empire, however, she returned to Vienna with her son, never to see the Emperor again.

Historical Provenance --- Empress Marie-Louise collection

Oil on canvas, gilt wood frame

### Sèvres teacup and saucer
Manufacture Imperiale de Sèvres
c. 1813

Empress Marie-Louise gave this unique cup and saucer bearing her likeness to the Duchess of Montebello, who looked after the King of Rome, Napoléon's son and heir.

Porcelain

### Empress Marie-Louise's silk finery basket
Brocard c. 1810

Servants brought cases such as this to Marie-Louise each morning. They held her personal belongings, such as handkerchiefs, jewelry and gold boxes.

Silk with gold thread

### Empress Marie-Louise's watch
Etienne Nitot (today: Chaumet) --- c. 1810

Empress Marie-Louise gave this watch as a thank-you gift to the French Consul in Turin, where she stopped on her way to Austria following Napoléon's first abdication in 1814.

Enamel, pearls and gold

## Study for "The King of Rome"

Baron François Gérard --- 1812

After a difficult labor, Empress Marie-Louise gave birth to a son, the King of Rome, on March 20, 1811. Napoléon had told the attending doctors that if it became a choice between mother and baby, they should save his wife. He was a doting father who was inordinately proud of his heir. Because his son had French and Austrian blood, Napoléon believed he would reconcile the two countries. Napoléon received the painting for which this drawing was a study while in Russia on September 6, 1812, the day before the Battle of Moskowa. He was very pleased with the portrait and exhibited it in his tent for others to admire. While staying at the Kremlin, he placed the image in his bedroom.

Historical Provenance --- Baron François Gérard family collection
Graphite on paper

## Bust of the King of Rome

Philipp Jakob Treu --- c. 1812

This is the only known sculpture of the son born to Napoléon and Marie-Louise in 1811, Napoléon François Joseph Charles, known as Napoléon II and the King of Rome. "King of Rome" is the traditional title for the heir to the Holy Roman Emperor.

Historical Provenance --- Caroline Murat family collection
Bronze on marble base

## Moulding of the King of Rome's hand

Made by Dubois, Empress Marie-Louise's doctor --- c. 1814

This cast was made at about the time that Napoléon saw his son for the last time, at the end of January 1814.

Historical Provenance --- Dubois family collection
Plaster

## "The King of Rome"

Innocent-Louis Goubaud --- c. 1812

In this portrait, Napoléon's baby son is surrounded by an ermine-trimmed cloak, a crown and other emblems of imperial authority. He confidently plays with a necklace of imperial eagles.

Engraving on vellum

## "The King of Rome"

Jean-Baptiste Isabey --- c. 1812

The portrait was presented to Madame de Montesquiou, the King of Rome's housekeeper, by the Empress Marie-Louise.

Watercolor on paper in silver gilt frame

## "Duke of Reichstadt"

Louis Léopold Boilly, after Daffinger --- c. 1830

After Napoléon's downfall, his son was taken back to the court of his grandfather, Francis II, in Vienna. There he was renamed Duke of Reichstadt and carefully tutored in Hapsburg history and culture. Although he hoped to someday have a realm of his own, he was to die of tuberculosis in July 1832 at the age of 21.

Historical Provenance --- Monstesquiou collection

Indian ink on paper

# The Imperial Court

apoléon created the Empire with the help of military colleagues and supporters, and he depended on them to help rule it. Some of his core circle of generals, whom he made Marshals of the Empire, were at his side from his early years to the final battle at Waterloo. Most of the Napoléon's friends remained loyal to the end, although a small number of his most renowned generals and counselors, like Foreign Minister Charles Maurice de Talleyrand-Perigord and General Jean Bernadotte, became notorious for their betrayal.

Although the Emperor lived in surroundings that befit his title, he maintained many of his Spartan ways. He never ceased to drive himself and those around him tirelessly, accomplishing a phenomenal amount in just a few years. Some, however, who surrounded him, including Joséphine, Talleyrand and his close, long-time advisor Jean Jacques Cambacérès, gained a reputation for their taste for the high life and fine food.

## "Marshal Louis Alexandre Berthier"
Alix, after Baron Antoine-Jean Gros — 1797
It is doubtful whether the French military command system would have functioned to the degree of excellence it did under Napoléon without Marshall Louis Berthier, his indispensable chief of staff. A veteran of the American Revolution, Berthier's brilliance lay in his ability to translate the Emperor's quick, decisive orders into easily understood messages to subordinates. During campaigns, he worked in the Emperor's eight-horse coach, which was like a mobile hotel, rarely leaving his side. He was with Napoléon from the First Italian Campaign in 1797 until just before the Battle of Waterloo in 1815, when he was either murdered or committed suicide.
Historical Provenance — Marshall Nicholas Soult collection
Engraving with watercolor

LE GÉNÉRAL BERTHIER.

« Je ne dois pas oublier l'intrépide Berthier qui a été dans cette journée Canonier, Cavalier et Grenadier. »
Extrait de la relation de Buonaparte sur la bataille de Lodi.

## Tableware belonging to Charles Maurice de Talleyrand-Périgord, seen with a bottle of Napoléon's brandy

Plates: Nast Manufacture, Paris. Forks: Lorillon

Talleyrand was the Minister of Foreign Affairs for Napoléon and a key diplomat in Europe at the time. He was famous for his skills as a political operative and his ability to represent his own interests and to accumulate wealth. Usually a perceptive judge of character, Napoléon never realized the extent of Talleyrand's disloyalty and deception.

Historical Provenance --- Talleyrand family collection from the Castle at Valençay
Porcelain, crystal and silver

## Charles-Maurice de Talleyrand-Périgord's prayer chair

Jacob Frère

This prayer chair, or prie-dieu, is a relic of Talleyrand's years as Bishop of Autun, prior to the French Revolution, and of his years of international diplomacy and intrigue. By the end of his life, he turned towards religion again and displayed this prayer chair in his bedroom.

Historical Provenance --- Rochecotte Castle
Sculpted and gilded wood with upholstery

## "Charles-Maurice de Talleyrand-Périgord"

Pierre-Paul Prudhon; engraving by Chapuy --- c. 1805
As in Shakespeare's play, Talleyrand consistently played *Iago* to Napoléon's *Othello,* deceiving him and selling him out from first to last. A consummate political actor, Talleyrand appears to have taken Napoléon in with his piety from his days as Bishop of Autun and his horror of wrongdoing in others.
Historical Provenance --- Castle of Valençay collection
Engraving

CHARLES MAURICE DE            TALLEYRAND PÉRIGORD,

## Sketch for the painting "Le Belleser" (Belisarius)

Baron François Gérard --- c. 1805-6
Baron Gérard dedicated this sketch to Talleyrand. It depicts 6th-century General Belisarius, who was one of the greatest military leaders of his time. His success brought him enemies though, and he was incriminated in a plot against the Emperor Justinian. For this, Belisarius was ordered blinded and stripped of all his possessions, reducing him to a beggar in the streets of Byzantium, where he had once commanded Roman armies.
Historical Provenance --- Castle of Valençay collection

## "Charles Maurice de Talleyrand-Périgord"

Jean-Baptiste Isabey --- c. 1795
A man of great culture and diplomatic ability, Talleyrand played a major role in Napoléon's foreign policy. Unfortunately, his avarice matched his diplomatic skills, so he increasingly played a double role, representing the interests of France's enemies at the same time that he was negotiating on behalf of the Emperor.
Historical Provenance --- Prince Joachim Murat collection
Graphite on paper

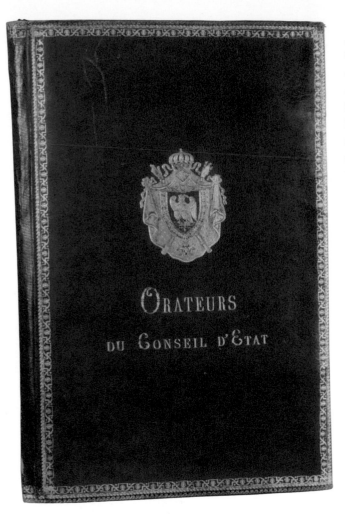

## Napoléon's portfolio inscribed "Orateurs Du Conseil d'Etat"

c. 1805

Napoléon regularly attended the meetings of the Council of State, at which important decisions were made regarding France's administration. Before and after the meetings, all documents, speeches and minutes were placed in this portfolio. Napoléon's coat of arms is on the front and back.

Red Morocco with green sillk

## Doodle drawn by Napoléon

Napoléon Bonaparte --- c. 1806

Abstract ink drawing reminiscent of a spider's web done on a letter from Tuileries. It is rare for any personal scribbles such as this to survive, as most were disposed of at the time.

Historical Provenance --- Berlioz collection

Indian ink on paper

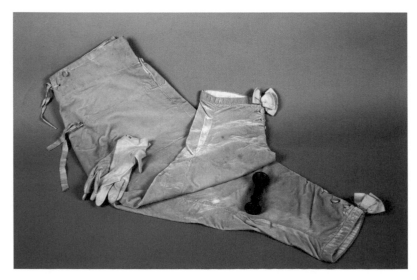

## General Henri-Gratien Bertrand's breeches and gloves

c. 1812-1815

General Bertrand managed the Imperial household during Napoléon's reign, and accompanied him into exile on Elba Island and later, St. Helena Island. He was the main executor of the Emperor's will. Worn on ceremonial occasions, these breeches (or culottes) were part of his official uniform as Grand Marshal of the Palace.

Historical Provenance --- Bertrand family collection

Lyon Velvet

## Account book of the Emperor's palaces

c. 1810-1811

This ledger contains all of the Imperial palaces' expenses, including the manufacture of furniture, aquisition of works of art and other purchases. Throughout can be found calculations and corrections in Napoléon's hand, reflecting his ability to guide an Empire of millions, while overseeing the day-to-day workings of his own household.

Historical Provenance --- Marshal Duroc collection

## Napoléon's lotto game box

Martin Guillaume Biennais --- c. 1810

Napoléon loved to play lotto with Joséphine and in later years, Marie-Louise. It was one of his favorite games. He wanted so passionately to win that, legend has it, he would sometimes "discover" cards in his sleeve. This game box, from the Palace at Fontainebleau, is the only one to survive.

Historical Provenance --- Former Siméon collection

Ebony, mahogany, silk, silver thread, painted horn

### Door latches from Napoléon's personal Tuileries apartment

These latches bear the Emperor's monogram and hint at the splendor of the apartment behind the doors they secured.

Gilded bronze

### Bust of Napoléon

Giuseppe Rocchi — c. 1810

Owned by Grand Marshal Bertrand, this image could easily be mistaken for that of an Emperor of the ancient Roman Empire, a time which Napoléon avidly studied and which greatly influenced his vision for his new Empire.

Historical Provenance — Bertrand family collection

Marble

## Chair from Napoléon's personal Tuileries office

This is one of just a handful of chairs that were used in the inner sanctum of the Empire, Napoléon's small, private office overlooking the Tuileries Gardens and the Seine. Here the Emperor, his private secretary and his intimate circle of advisors sat during the years they worked tirelessly to rebuild France and change the face of Europe.

Napoléon normally dictated his correspondence, sometimes simultaneously composing multiple letters with the assistance of several secretaries. With great focus, he spoke quickly, moving from secretary to secretary, often running far ahead of their shorthand. Afterwards, he would make corrections on transcripts he was provided and finally sign the polished documents.

Historical Provenance — Olivier Lefuel collection
Gilded wood, velvet and brocade

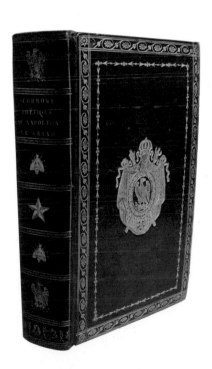

## Books from the Emperor's libraries

A voracious reader, Napoléon amassed an inventory of thousands of volumes throughout his life. This book, *Couronne Poétique* (poetic crown) *of Napoléon the Great 1807,* is from the Emperor's libraries at the Tuileries.

Green Morocco leather and paper

# Art & the Emperor

apoléon believed in the power of the arts as a propaganda tool and supported them to glorify his reign and the new Empire he had established. He used the arts to promote the view that France was carrying on the traditions of the Roman Republic and the Holy Roman Empire and that he was the new Julius Caesar or Charlemagne. Napoléon was also interested in encouraging the industrial arts as a means of building a new business infrastructure for France. Focusing on everything from the production of silk to the construction of civic edifices, from furniture manufacturing to silver smithing, he used the arts to grow the French economy. Napoléon had great vision for a new, improved Paris and was responsible for commissioning many of the grand boulevards and monuments that make the city what it is today.

"Marie Thérèse Bourgoin"
Henri François Riesener
An actress at the Comédie Française, Mademoiselle Bourgoin briefly became the mistress of Napoléon and later of Tsar Alexander I. Bourgoin was said to have impugned the Emperor's virility. He later denied having had an affair with her.

Recently Museum specialists have speculated that this work may have been painted by one of the great artists of the era, Jacques-Louis David, while he was in exile in Brussels in 1814. Riesener worked with David, and the latter was a friend of, and had previously painted, Bourgoin.
Oil on Canvas

"Napoléon I"
Antonio Canova — c. 1810
Napoléon had a great fondness for art that recalled the glory of the Roman empire. In Canova's portrait, he is depicted as a Roman emperor. The image shows the toll that worry and constant warfare is taking on him, although he is only 41.
Historical Provenance — Bertrand family collection
Charcoal and graphite on paper

### Relief portrait of Napoléon
Antonio Canova — 1809
Canova was a talented sculptor who dedicated his career to reviving the classical style of art, as in this profile of Napoléon as a Roman emperor, wearing a laurel crown. His most famous work is the great reclining nude "Venus Victrix," for which Pauline Borghese, Napoléon's favorite sister, posed.
Bisque

## Study for "The Intervention of the Sabine Women"
Jacques-Louis David —- c. 1794-99
David is reputed to have painted *The Intervention of the Sabine Women,* with its theme of love prevailing over conflict, to honor his wife who divorced him during the Revolution. He began it while he was in prison. This work reestablished his fortunes and brought him to the attention of Napoléon, who appointed David his official painter.

## Study for "The Intervention of the Sabine Women"
Edme Gratien Parizeau for Jacques-Louis David —- c. 1799
One of David's students, Parizeau collaborated on several of his mentor's painting including *The Intervention of the Sabine Women.* Napoléon influenced the arts not only through his personal tastes, but also through his military successes. The combination of these two factors resulted in the Empire style.
Graphite on paper

## Fight scene
Horace Vernet —- c. 1810
Two warriors have competed in front of their opposing armies. One now stands with a broken sword in hand, dragging his adversary who remains unharmed. Here again, a classical theme provides a vehicle for creative expression.
Historical Provenance —- Paul Delaroche collection
Indian ink and gouache on paper

## "Colossal Bust of Napoléon"
Antonio Canova — c. 1810

In 1802, Napoléon brought Italian neoclassical sculptor Antonio Canova to Paris to model his portrait in marble. Canova carved the Colossal Bust as a study for a monumental, full-length statue, *Napoléon as Mars the Peacemaker*. Napoléon disliked the nudity of the completed statue and would not approve it for public installation. Nevertheless, the bust was still greatly admired for its Olympian size and power to evoke the busts of antiquity. As a result, Canova, his students and the Carrara sculptors made numerous copies, including the one in this exhibition.

This bust was in the collection of Louis-Philippe (King of France 1830-1848). It suffered major damage during the British bombing of the King's Normandy country-palace during the Nazi occupation in World War II.

Historical Provenance — French Royal Collection, Property of King Louis-Philippe

Marble

## Medici-style vases
Louis-François Jeannest — c. 1811-1812

With the demand for bronze to cast cannons, large-scale artworks in this alloy of tin and copper were rarely made during the time. These two are the only known bronze vases of the period on this scale. Depicted in a classical motif, they represent Napoléon's marriage to Marie-Louise and the King of Rome's birth in 1811. Napoléon's eagle, bee and heroic symbolism feature prominently, as well.

Historical Provenance — Ordered by Napoléon, Murat collection

Bronze

## Fabric sample from Versailles

Grand-Frères (silk manufacturer of Lyons) — c. 1810-1811

In honor of his marriage to the Archduchess Marie-Louise of Austria in April 1810, Napoléon redecorated Versailles, placing numerous orders for silk fabrics from Grand-Frères. This fabric sample, from the palace's great living room, includes his personal emblem, the bee, as well as images related to the glories of the Roman Empire.
Silk

## Preparatory drawing for "Psyche and Cupid" ▶

François Gérard — c. 1798

The neoclassic style of the First Empire often celebrated the beauties of the nude body, sometimes straining the limits of credibility. In this study for a painting that hangs in the Louvre, Baron Gérard pursues the perfection of physical beauty through line, composition, color and the delicate rendering of flesh.

Historical Provenance — Bulot collection
Graphite on paper

## Busts of Napoléon and Marie-Louise

Baron François Joseph Bosio — c. 1812

In addition to his bronze portraits of the Imperial family, Bosio, a master in the medium, was employed by Napoléon to make the bas-reliefs for the sculptor Pierre-Nolasque Bergeret's monument, the 144 foot-high Place Vendôme column. Modeled after Trajan's column in Rome, the spiral veneer surrounding the stone structure, was cast from the cannons confiscated after the Battle of Austerlitz.
Bronze

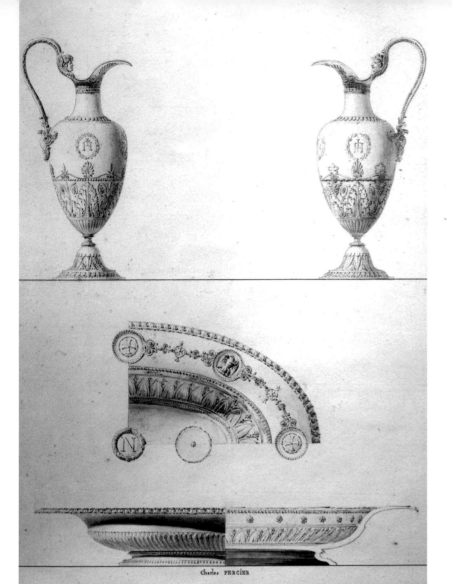

## Sketch of cruets and tray used at the Emperor's coronation

Charles Percier --- 1804

Many beautiful objects were required to assist in the anointing in oil, washing of hands, dispersal of incense, reading of texts and so forth during the coronation.

Historical Provenance --- The Percier collection

Indian ink on paper

## Silver service of Jean Jacques Cambacérès, Second Consul and Archchancellor of the Empire

Martin-Guillaume Biennais

Cambacérès was renowned throughout Paris for the sumptuousness of his table, where guests enjoyed in reverent silence such delicacies as partridges roasted on one side and grilled on the other. By contrast, Napoléon preferred roast chicken and other simple fare, accompanied by watered wine.

Silver

## Plate with view of the Hôtel de Ville (City Hall of Paris)

Robert —- c. 1806

Presented by Napoléon to Jean Jacques Cambacérès on the occasion of his niece's wedding, this plate is from an 80+ piece service. It depicts the Hôtel de Ville, the city hall of Paris, where the Emperor would have celebrations for both his coronation and his marriage to Marie-Louise. This is one of the few views of the Hôtel de Ville from the period.

Historical Cambacérès family collection
Manufacture Imperiale de Sèvres

## Sketch of a pavilion for Napoléon I's coronation festivities

Charles Percier and Pierre François Léonard Fontaine —- 1804

All of Paris was taken up with the coronation festivities on December 2, 1804, and Percier and Fontaine designed dramatic, temporary structures across the city. This pavilion was erected in the gardens of the Tuileries.

Pen, ink and watercolor on paper

# Napoléon at War

apoléon Bonaparte ranks among the greatest military strategists and field commanders who ever lived. He repeatedly defeated much larger armies by duping enemy generals into dividing up their forces and using flanking maneuvers that required unheard of speed and precision of troop movement. His structure for the Grand Army facilitated the command and deployment of vast forces and is used to this day. The names of his victorious battles continue to resonate— Austerlitz, Marengo, Wagram, Arcola, Jena. Because of his successes and his ability to appeal to their honor, Napoléon evoked fierce loyalty from his troops, in spite of the fact that the persistent attacks of his enemies, combined with his own ambition, caused him to sacrifice the lives of hundreds of thousands of French fighting men during his years in power.

## Bonaparte Crossing the Alps by the Great Saint Bernard Pass

Jean-Baptiste Mauzaisse after Jacques-Louis David ― c. 1807
The most famous depiction of Napoléon's military career, Bonaparte Crossing the Alps captures the energy and excitement of his Italian campaigns and rise to power. Like Hannibal and Charlemagne, whose names appear at the painting's bottom, Bonaparte courageously took his forces over the Alps in order to surprise his enemy. The strategy ultimately secured him victory at the Battle of Marengo. This painting also demonstrates David's talent as a propagandist for Napoléon, who actually crossed the mountains on a mule.
Oil on canvas

## "Napoléon in Uniform"

Baron Pierre-Narcisse Guérin --- c. 1811

By 1810, Napoléon had been at war almost constantly for 15 years. He had administered an empire of more than 80 million inhabitants, with unrelenting attention to detail, for 10 years. Although he was still near the top of his game, the effects of so much stress are beginning to show.

Drawing on vellum paper, with gouache

## "Surrender of the City of Ulm"

Carle Vernet --- c. 1806-17

On October 20,1805, the Austrian forces, forming part of the Third Coalition with England, Naples and Russia, surrendered to Napoléon. He took 33,000 prisoners and captured 60 cannons and 40 flags. A month later, Napoléon entered Vienna, without opposition or fanfare. His resounding defeat of the Russian army at Austerlitz on December 2, 1805, spelled the end of the coalition.

Sepia on paper

## "The Battle of Wagram"

Carle Vernet

The Battle of Wagram in early July 1809 was Napoléon's last great military victory. Once again, he demonstrated an ability to instantly assess battlefield developments and act decisively. But it was nearly a fiasco, and was one of the bloodiest battles in history, costing 34,000 French and 50,000 Austrian lives. One historian has called Wagram "two days of competitive homicide."

Historical Provenance --- Countess de Chambure collection

Indian ink with gouache on paper

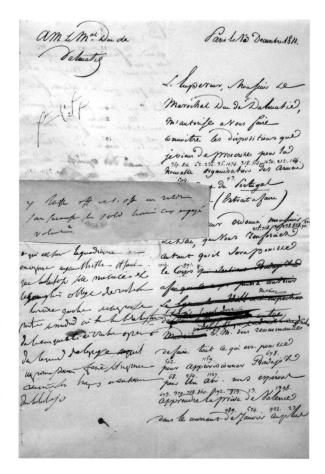

### Order to defend Madrid sent from Napoléon

Emperor Napoléon I --- December 1811

Napoléon invaded Portugal in 1807 as part of his initiative to close ports that the British used for trade. He then invaded Bourbon-ruled Spain, wishing in large measure to spread the ideals of the Revolution. Unlike the Italians, the fiercely patriotic Spaniards did not take to French rule. Resistance remained strong and occupied the attention of 300,000 troops that Napoléon sorely needed elsewhere.

Ink on paper

75

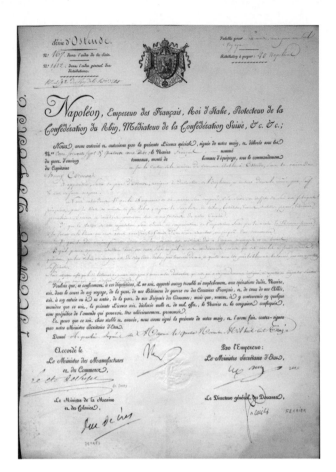

## Boat license granted by the Emperor during the Continental Blockade

c. 1813

The plan to bring England to its knees by stifling her trade was a good one, but, unfortunately, Europe was much too porous and complex for it to be truly effective. The other problem was that everyone prized English goods. Napoléon sometimes ignored the blockade himself to purchase luxuries for Joséphine.

*Engraving with ink on paper*

## Soldier of the Imperial Guard

Nicolas-Toussaint Charlet

Napoléon drew from his crack regiments to form the Imperial Guard. Although they were the best soldiers the army could provide, he kept them in reserve in battle after battle. Some historians feel that this accounts for the regiment's lackluster performance at Waterloo, when they finally had a chance to enter the fray.

*India Ink on paper*

## Portfolio and writing case of General Jean Rapp

Rapp was one of the architects of the victory at Austerlitz in December 1805. The Emperor's aide-de-camp at the time, he was appointed major general a few days after the battle.

*Green and silver Morocco leather*

## Napoléon's personal map of the French Empire in 1812

c. 1812

Napoléon's personal map of the French Empire in 1812, with pin pricks attributed to him, marking his campaigns. "It was a beautiful Empire!" he reminisced on St. Helena. "I had eighty-three million human beings under my government—half the population of Europe."

Paper lined with silk

## "Grenadier of the Guard"

Hippolyte Bellangé --- 1859

The Grenadiers of the Guard were part of Napoléon's elite Imperial Guard. This depiction shows a guardsman during his final campaign in Belgium in 1815.

Watercolor and pastel on paper

## Convertible armchair of Marshal Louis Nicolas Davout

c. 1808

This armchair that converts into a bed belonged to Louis Nicolas Davout, who accompanied Napoléon to Egypt and in the Second Italian Campaign, becoming a Marshal in 1804. He also participated in the Russian campaign, and was Minister of War during the Hundred Days between Napoléon's escape from Elba and his defeat at Waterloo.

Historical Provenance --- Marshal Louis Nicolas Davout collection
Steel with brass fittings

## Saucepan from Napoléon's campaign set

This pan, engraved with an "N" under the Imperial crown and "Voyages," was used during the Emperor's travels in the Vendée region.

Copper

## Napoléon's collapsible campaign bed

Desouches --- c. 1808

"The strength of an army, like the amount of momentum in mechanics, is estimated by the mass times the velocity," said Napoléon. When on campaign, he moved as quickly as his soldiers did, sleeping exclusively on collapsible, easily transportable beds such as this. Commissioned in 1808, it was probably used at the Battle of Wagram.

Historical Provenance --- Bertrand family collection

# The Road to Defeat

Although Napoléon's army was almost universally victorious and his empire grew to govern more than 80 million people, these gains proved to be short-lived. The fierce resistance of Spain to French rule, a series of international coalitions formed to defeat the "upstart" French Emperor, a disastrous decision to invade Russia, the war weariness of his Marshals and his inability to rally occupied Paris led to his abdication at Fontainebleau in 1814. He was exiled to Elba and Bourbon rule was restored under King Louis XVIII. Napoléon's exile did not last long, however. Within less than a year, he escaped from Elba and returned to France, rallying the French people to his side in yet another bloodless coup. During the "Hundred Days," Napoléon continued to wage war with his enemies, now more determined than ever to eliminate this threat to their monarchies. Final defeat came at the hands of generals Wellington and Blücher on the battlefield at Waterloo, a name that has become synonymous with personal downfall.

"Napoléon at Fontainebleau"
Paul Hippolyte Delaroche — 1848
One of the most famous events in the Napoléon canon is his moving farewell to the Grand Army at Fontainebleau after his first abdication in 1814. The advent of Louis-Philippe as king of France in 1830 encouraged the resurgence of the cult of Napoléon. Paul Delaroche became a well known interpreter of the legend.
Historical Provenance — Private collection, Belgium
Oil on canvas

### "Moscow Burning"

1813

The destruction of Moscow during the French occupation in September 1812 was among the many tragedies of the ill-conceived Russian campaign. Although the fire's origins have never been proven, it is likely that the Russian army set fire to the city, preferring to burn it down than have it occupied by the French.

Engraving with watercolor and gouache on paper

### Preparatory study for a head of a wounded soldier

Théodore Géricault — 1817

The suffering was unfathomable during the retreat from Russia in 1812 as the Grand Army slogged through the icy Russian winter with Cossacks ambushing and killing them at every turn. Without Marshall Ney's brilliant rearguard action, the entire army might have been lost. As it was, of the more than 530,000 men estimated to have left for Russia, only a few thousand returned.

Graphite on paper

## The Napoleonic Wars through English eyes

English engravings — c. 1813-14

These propagandistic English engravings from a larger set depict the horrors of the Grand Army's retreat from Russia, as well as Napoléon's flight in disguise. Though slanted, they are not far from the truth.

Engraving embellished with watercolor

"The Retreat of the French Army from Russia at the Battle of Leipzig"

"Miseries of the French Grand Army"

"Bonaparte's Flight in Disguise"

### Emperor's horse Tauris

Carle Vernet --- c. 1810

Napoléon owned and used over 150 horses during the course of his life, 19 of which were shot out from under him. Tauris, a silvery grey, slightly dappled Persian, was a gift from Tsar Alexander I. Napoléon rode him at the battles of Vitebsk, Smolensk and Borodino, during his entrance into Moscow, and during the retreat from Russia. He also rode him from the coast of France to Paris during the Hundred Days.

Of his equestrian skills, Napoléon's valet Constant wrote, "The Emperor mounted a horse without grace... and I believe that he would not have always been very sturdy on the horse if we had not taken so much care to give him only horses perfectly trained." Similarly, Ernst Otto Odeleben wrote, "Napoléon rode like a butcher...whilst galloping, his body rolled backwards and forwards and sideways, according to the speed of his horse."

Historical Provenance --- Marshal Koenig collection

India ink on paper

### "The French Campaign"

Ernest Meissonier --- c. 1861

Finally, in 1814, what Napoléon had struggled to avoid for years came to pass—the war came home to France. He tried to rally his troops for a heroic defense of the motherland and won battles at Champaubert, Montmirail and elsewhere, but nearly 20 years of battles had taken their toll. The country desperately wanted peace.

Engraving

## "Marshal Lefèbvre Presenting the Abdication Act to Napoléon"

Etienne Prosper Bellecour --- c. 1860

Direct and honest, Marshal François Joseph Lefèbvre remained loyal to the First Consul and Emperor to the end. Though he supported Napoléon's 1814 abdication, he was by his side again when the Emperor returned to power for the Hundred Days prior to the Battle of Waterloo.

Graphite on paper

## Napoléon's farewell to Pierre de Montesquiou

Emperor Napoléon I --- 1814

In this letter, Napoléon bids goodbye to Pierre de Montesquiou, Grand Chamberlain of France, before signing his abdication and departing for Elba. He wrote it on April 14, 1814, the morning after his suicide attempt.

Historical Provenance --- de Montesquiou family collection
Ink on paper

## Armchair from Fontainebleau Palace

Pierre-Benoit Marcion; gilding by Chatard (the Emperor's gilder) --- 1809

Fontainebleau was one of Napoléon's favorite residences. Although he was not given to great pomp and ceremony, he knew the value of luxury in impressing his subjects. As he said, "A newly established government must dazzle and astonish." No grandeur however, could ease the crushing blow of losing his beloved Empire and all that he had worked to achieve.

Gilded wood and lacquer

## Duke of Massa's portfolio

The Duke of Massa presided over the legislative body that voted to depose Napoléon in 1814.

Historical Provenance --- Duc of Massa collection

Red Morocco leather with silver

## "The Congress of Vienna"

Godefroy Engelmann, after Jean-Baptiste Isabey --- 1819

At the Congress of Vienna from September 1814 to June 1815, the leaders of England, Europe and Russia met to discuss the fate of Napoléon and the French Empire.

Historical Provenance --- Valençay Castle collection

Engraving on paper

## "King Louis XVIII"

c. 1814

An unimaginative and inept ruler, Louis XVIII, wasted little time in reinstituting many of the privileges of the ancient régime after his ascendancy in 1814. When Napoléon escaped from Elba in 1815, the King fled, refusing to even try to defend Paris.

Oil on canvas

## Louis XVIII medallion design (detail)

Carle Vernet

Vernet designed this emblem for the throne room of the king. Though a Bourbon, Louis XVIII loved the Empire style and employed many of the artists previously used by Napoléon.

Watercolor on canvas

## Preliminary drawing for Louis XVIII's coat of arms

Carle Vernet — c. 1814-15

Fabric based on this design was probably used in the throne room at the Tuileries.

Historical Provenance —
Picot collection

Watercolor and gouache on canvas parchment

## Eagle of the Hundred Days
### (1815)

During the "Hundred Days" between Napoléon's escape from exile on the Island of Elba and his final defeat at Waterloo, the Imperial symbol of the eagle took on added significance. Legend has it that eagles began to circle overhead from the moment the Emperor landed at Golfe-Juan on the Riviera, and continued to do so throughout his journey to Paris.

Gilded wood

## Officer's shako worn by Grenadiers of the 93th Regiment
### c. 1812

This regiment participated in the Russian campaign of 1812 and the Battle of Waterloo in 1815.

## Cannonballs and grapeshot from the battlefield at Waterloo

On June 18, 1815, 191,300 soldiers fought at Waterloo, one of history's most decisive and analyzed battles. Some 72,000 French faced 67,000 troops commanded by Britain's Duke of Wellington and another 53,000 under Prussia's General Blücher. The debate will continue forever as to what might have changed the course of events, but at the end of the day, 48,000 men were killed or severely wounded, and Blücher and Wellington had achieved final victory over Napoléon.

Historical Provenance — Waterloo Battlefield collection

## Silver cutlery and cup

Martin-Guillaume Biennais — 1798-1809

Napoléon used these items at his last battle—Waterloo, on June 18, 1815. They were retrieved from the Emperor's personal carriage by Marshal Gebhard von Blücher. It is very rare for any of Napoléon's personal silver to survive; most of it was melted down following the restoration of the Bourbons.

Historical Provenance — Marshal Blücher collection

Vermeil, silver and metal

# The Final Exile

**A**fter his second abdication, Napoléon surrendered to the English, hoping that he could retire to the English countryside. However, his captors were taking no chances that their prisoner would once again return to his throne. They exiled him to St. Helena, a remote and barren island in the South Atlantic. A small party of the most loyal members of his staff and of the Imperial Court, including General Henri-Gratien Bertrand, accompanied him to this dismal outpost, a hell on earth for men who were "addicts of action." The island's celebrated prisoner chaffed under the authority of English Governor Hudson Lowe, a situation made even more unpleasant by their mutual dislike for each other. The fallen Emperor spent his time reading, gardening, dictating his memoirs and ruminating on the remarkable events that had led him to St. Helena.

"The Last Stage"
James Sant ⸺ c. 1900
This portrait was commissioned for the historical monograph *Napoléon: The Last Phase,* one of several histories written by Lord Rosebery, Queen Victoria's Prime Minister in 1894-95. It eloquently testifies to how much the years of struggle and ill health had affected Napoléon by the time he arrived at St. Helena.
Historical Provenance ⸺ Private collection, England
Oil on canvas

## "Bonaparte on St. Helena Island"

January 16, 1816

The first published engraving of Napoléon at St. Helena shows him standing in front of The Briars, the residence of William Balcombe, the East India Company agent. Napoléon became very fond of the family, particularly of 14-year-old Betsy, who, with the innocence of youth, treated him as an equal. She frequently pointed out that he cheated at cards.

Engraving on paper

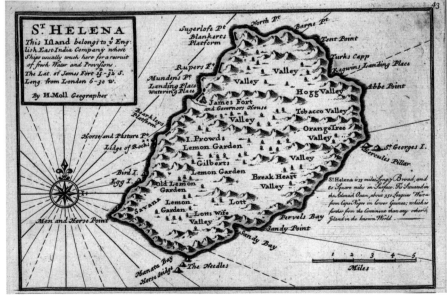

## Map of St. Helena Island

17th century

Used as a watering stop for East India Company ships and as a location from which the Royal Navy could dominate the South Atlantic, St. Helena was a mountainous tropical island a mere 28 miles in circumference. The nearest land, the west coast of Africa, was 1,140 miles away. A "buoy lost in the South Atlantic," it was hell on earth for a man of Napoléon's active temperament.

Ink on paper

## General Henri-Gratien Bertrand's box
Martin Guillaume Biennais

General Bertrand was one of four friends who chose to share Napoléon's exile. The others were General Tristan de Montholon, General Gaspard Gourgaud and Count Emmanuel de Las Cases. Also accompanying the Emperor in exile were Fanny Bertrand and Albine de Montholon, his friends' loyal wives. After Napoléon's death, General Bertrand filled this box with souvenirs of the Emperor before leaving St. Helena.

Historical Provenance --- Duc de Padou collection

Mahogany, brass, silk, green morocco

## "View of Buonaparte's New Mansion"
From *A Traveller's Notebook, or From Buonaparte to Longwood* --- 1819

After a few months in Jamestown, the port of St. Helena, Napoléon was moved five miles away to Longwood, a converted farmhouse at 1,700 feet elevation. Here he would spend the last five and a half years of his life in a suite of rooms comprising a study, drawing room, antechamber, bathroom and bedroom. Napoléon received this book about himself while in exile in 1820.

Historical Provenance --- Napoléon's library, Bertrand family collection

Colored engraving on paper

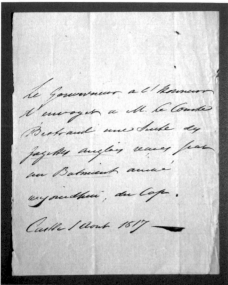

## Letter from Sir Hudson Lowe to Grand Marshal Bertrand
Hudson Lowe --- August 1817

This letter was sent with English newspapers. Napoléon was eager to receive these newspapers which remained his only source of information about the outside world.

Historical Provenance --- Hudson Lowe family collection

Ink on paper

## "Bonaparte on St. Helena Island"
Jean-Pierre Marie Jazet --- c. 1825

Napoléon and his small entourage, presumably here being shown their barren new home by the red-coated British captors, did their best to pass the time and relieve the boredom by taking walks, playing cards and dining at the Emperor's table.

Engraving on paper

## Architectural rendering

Princesse Charlotte Bonaparte
1819

Given to him by his niece Charlotte, this was one of the few
gifts sent to Napoléon on St.
Helena. Charlotte and her sister,
Zenaïde, were the daughters of
Napoléon's brother Joseph and
Julie Clary. The Emperor was
very touched to receive this
drawing from Charlotte, who
was then 17 years old.

Sepia ink on paper

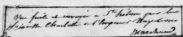

## Lock of Napoléon's hair

During Napoléon's lifetime, his personal possessions were already
becoming regarded as treasured relics of a great man. On St.
Helena, while he was having his hair cut one day, the Emperor
noticed his friend Count Emmanuel de Las Cases hiding a bit of his
hair and asked him what he was doing. When Las Cases denied
doing anything, Napoléon simply gave him a wry smile.

Historical Provenance --- Las Casas family collection

### Napoléon's Madras kerchief worn on St. Helena

c. 1818-19

Due to the high humidity on the island, Napoléon preferred to wear a kerchief to cover his head rather than a felt hat. Joséphine introduced her husband to this West Indian custom. One can imagine him wearing this cloth while tending the garden that he started to plant in 1819, rising each day at 5:30 a.m.

Historical Provenance --- Abbot Vignali collection

Cotton

### Napoléon's monogrammed shirt and longjohns worn on St. Helena

Stained with blood, this is one of the last shirts worn by the Emperor on St. Helena.

Historical Provenance --- Bertrand family collection

### Napoléon's stockings worn on St. Helena

The stockings have an openwork "N" under the imperial crown.

Historical Provenance --- Comte de Montholon collection

Silk

### Napoléon's pencils used on St. Helena
The paper bears the Emperor's mathematical calculations in pencil.

Historical Provenance ---- Comte de Montholon collection

### Napoléon's toiletry items from St. Helena
Soap, toothpicks, toothpaste and pins with which he marked battle maps, all formed part of Napoléon's possessions at St. Helena.

Historical Provenance ---- Abbot Vignali collection

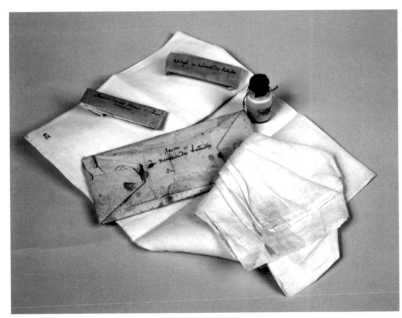

### Napoléon's flacon for smelling salts or perfume from St. Helena
Napoléon was fastidious about cleanliness. He began each day with an hour-long hot bath. He then shaved himself. Following that, he washed his hands with almond paste and his face, neck and ears with soap and water. Finally, he would strip to the waist and pour eau de cologne over his head and down his torso. This bottle was filled with violet-scented perfume.

Historical Provenance ---- Bertrand family collection
Crystal and silver gilt

## Emperor's tableware from St. Helena

Martin-Guillaume Biennais (knife) and Louis Nicolas Sommé (cutlery)

To keep up his spirits, Napoléon dined formally most evenings with his friends and their wives. Despite their remote exile, they initially ate well on St. Helena. Later, when the English informed him they were reducing his food budget from 20,000 to 12,000 pounds a year, he was outraged. Low on funds, Napoléon had basketsful of his silver service hammered down and sold to raise money for his table. He would do this three times in all, making these pieces all the rarer.

Historical Provenance — Given by Joseph Bonaparte to his nephew, Nicolas Clary

## Napoléon's campaign teabox used on St. Helena

Martin-Guillaume Biennais — c. 1805

As he had in his royal palaces, on St. Helena Napoléon liked to surround himself with the campaign equipment he had carried into battle.

Historical Provenance — Duc de Massa collection
Mahogany and gilded brass

98

## Book from St. Helena

This book is from the personal library of 1,600 volumes that Napoléon had at St. Helena. He said he needed at least 60,000 books to deal with the boredom he felt on the island. Several of the volumes bear English inscriptions. Much of his library was lost in the fire at the Tuileries Palace in 1871.

Napoléon received *Memoirs and Correspondence of Joséphine* before he died in March 1821, and read it just days before he became gravely ill. It was the only book he ever read about Joséphine and the questionable veracity of some of the content upset him greatly.

Historical Provenance --- Bertrand family collection

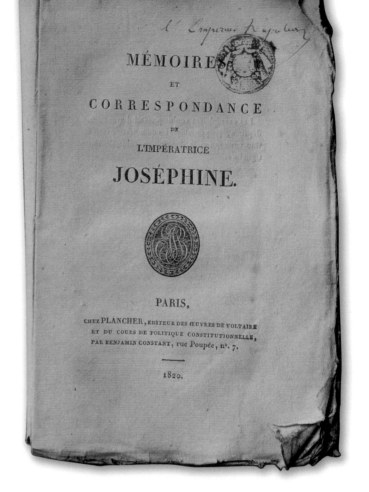

## A handwritten fragment of Napoléon's English lessons

1816

Part of Napoléon's English lessons with Count de Las Cases, this sheet includes several French sentences that he translated, such as, "Quand êtes-vous parti du Cap? When are you departed from the Cap?" Napoléon proved to be an indifferent linguist.

Historical Provenance --- Count Emmanuel de Las Cases collection

ink on paper

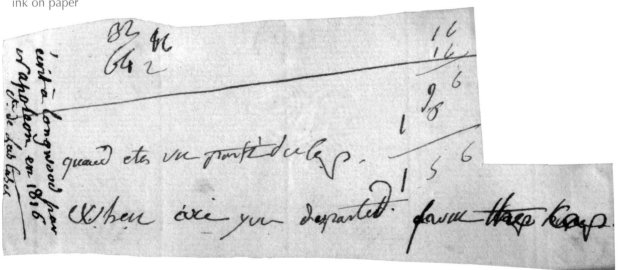

# Death of the Emperor

apoléon Bonaparte died in Longwood, his St. Helena home, on May 5, 1821, presumably of stomach cancer, although some have suggested that he was assassinated, possibly by poison mixed into his wine. He was interred on the island until 1840, when the English government allowed his remains to be returned to Paris and placed in the chapel of Les Invalides, a hospital and home for war veterans. In 1861, the Emperor's majestic tomb under the dome of Les Invalides was completed and he came, at long last, to his final resting place next to the Seine, as he had requested.

"Napoléon in Uniform on His Deathbed"
Jean-Baptiste Mauzaisse c.1841
Napoléon is shown on his deathbed, dressed in his cere-monial uniform with his Legion of Honour medallion and hat. The artist was a friend of the Emperor's valet, Louis Joseph Marchand, who provided all the details necessary to complete the scene.
Oil on canvas

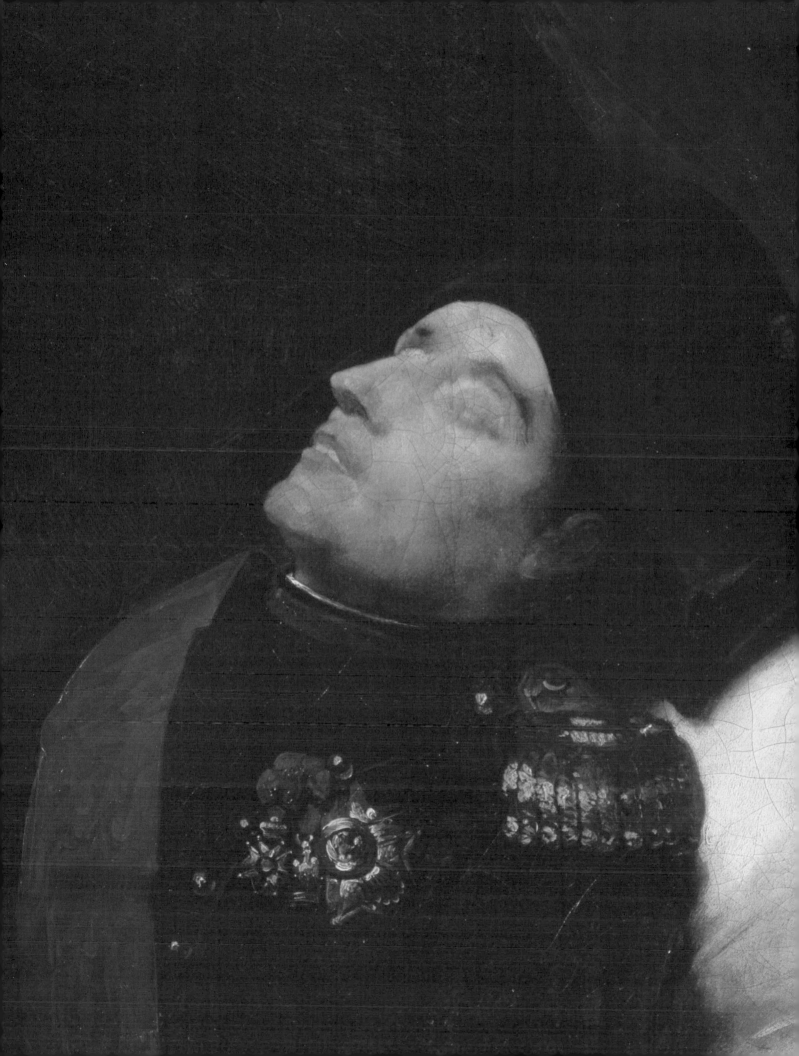

## "Napoléon I in Limbo"

Thérésa Tallien, Princesse de Chimay —— 1822

Thérésa Tallien was, like Joséphine, one of the beauties who ruled the Directory (1795-99) with the curve of their hips. Early in his reign, the prudish Napoléon encouraged her to leave Paris. She remained friends with Joséphine, however, visiting her frequently at Malmaison after her divorce.

Historical Provenance —— Princesse de Chimay collection
Drawing with India ink on paper

## Fragment of cloak worn by Napoléon at the Battle of Marengo

c. 1800

On his death, the cloak worn by Napoléon during one of his greatest victories was placed over his corpse. Captain J. W. Crossley later cut a piece as a souvenir. The remainder of the cloak was burnt in a fire in London in 1825, and this is believed to be the only surviving fragment.

Historical Provenance —— Lazarus collection
Wool cloth embroidered with gold thread

## Napoléon's first will, envelope, quill pen and desk blotter

August 1819

In his first will, written to General Bertrand in 1819, Napoléon makes generous bequests to the general and the other friends who accompanied him to St. Helena. He also instructs Bertrand to "take my silver, my armor, my porcelain, my books with Imperial Arms for my son, and everything that you think can be used one day."

Historical Provenance —— Bertrand family collection

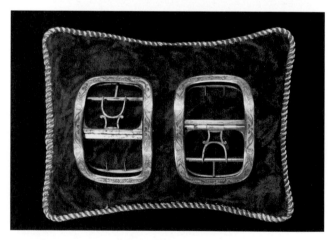

## Napoléon's shoe buckles worn on St. Helena

c. 1815

In his will, Napoléon mentions golden shoebuckles (he frequently referred to vermeil as gold, although it is actually gilded silver). All of his personal belongings were supposed to be handed over to his son, known then as the Duke of Reichstadt. His will was not respected, however, and his executors, Bertrand, Montholon and Noveraz, kept everything.

Historical Provenance —— Duc de Padoue collection
Vermeil silver

## Napoléon dying

c.1825

In his final days, Napoléon grew increasingly ill, suffering severe pains in his side and vomiting attacks. Knowing the end was near he asked his ashes be put "on the banks of the Seine, amongst the French people, whom I love so well." He also spoke over and over of his son. His last words were said to have been, "France, my son, the Army," while some also thought they heard him say, "Joséphine."

Engraving on paper

## "Napoléon Laid Out on His Austerlitz Camp Bed"

Captain Frederick Marryat —— May 6, 1821

Captain Frederick Marryat rendered this sketch 14 hours after Napoléon's passing. Marryat was temporary commander of the ship *Rosario,* which took the dispatches announcing the death to England.

Historical Provenance —— Frederick Marryat collection

Graphite on paper

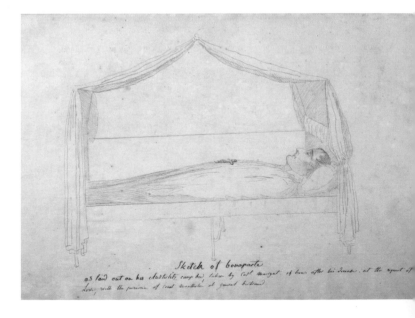

### Study for "Remains of Napoléon Leaving St. Helena"
Louis Gabriel Eugène Isabey — c.1840
On October 15, 1840, at 5:30 p.m., Napoléon's coffin was carried aboard La Belle Poule, anchored in Jamestown harbor. A single, brilliant star shown directly above the boat. Isabey later received a request from King Louis-Philippe to draw the scene, following the return of Napoléon's remains.
Gouache on paper

## Fragment of Napoléon's original coffin

1821

When the French government took Napoléon's body from St. Helena in 1840, they placed it in a new coffin. The original coffin was cut into pieces as souvenirs, of which General Bertrand got the largest section.

Historical Provenance ---- Bertrand family collection

Mahogany

## Logbook of Belle Poule

September-December 1840

Logbook of the Belle Poule, which returned Napoléon's remains to France from St. Helena in 1840. Personal copy of General Henri-Gratien Bertrand, who accompanied the voyage.

Historical Provenance ---- Bertrand family collection

# The Legend –
# Napoléon Lives On

apoléon was conscious of the impression he made and sought to control his image from the earliest days of his career until his imprisonment on St. Helena. A master of propaganda, he presented himself as a humble soldier and as royalty cloaked in ermines and jewels, depending upon his intentions. He burnished his image even further while at St. Helena, dictating his memoirs and at times, tailoring history to his advantage. His legend was beginning to take flight by then, and Napoléon read with interest of himself in materials about him that would make their way to his island exile.

Countless books and articles have delved into his story since his death, each author seeking to explain what sort of man believes he can change the world. The resulting portrait is complex and contradictory. The figure who emerges is a keen judge of character, who somehow trusted disloyal and double-crossing colleagues. A husband who deeply loved his wife but divorced her when she failed to produce an heir. A general who felt intensely about his soldiers, yet sacrificed hundreds of thousands of them during his military career, and although fearless, abandoned his men when he felt it expedient. A brilliant administrator who did everything he could to strengthen the French nation, while embroiling her in two decades of constant warfare. Endlessly fascinating, the true nature of Napoléon's character will be debated for centuries. Triumphant and tragic, his life captured the full breadth of human emotion, and his story rarely fails to evoke strong emotions in the telling, be they admiration or contempt or both.

The Emperor's Hat, summer model
seen with Napoléon's Legion of Honour Sash
Poupard Chapelier —— c.1805
There is no greater icon of the Napoléon legend than his hat. This one was worn in the 1809 Battle of Essling. He preferred the design "broadside on," the sides parallel with his shoulders, so that in battle, he could be distinguished from his officers, who wore their hats "fore-and-aft." The style and shape of his famous hat changed with the times, and the size was not always the same. Several examples, both summer and winter weight, have survived.
Historical Provenance —— General Mouton collection
Felt

To learn more about

# NAPOLÉON
## An Intimate Portrait

visit www.napoleonexhibit.com


For more information about and to become a member of the
**NAPOLEONIC SOCIETY OF AMERICA**
visit www.napoleonsociety.org